"I was pleased when ⸻ pleased when he finis⸻ with me to *Naviga*⸻ beginning, 'plunged i⸻ ⸻, to the closing, 'in the hands of the Father,' you will receive confidence and hope."

Maxie Dunnam, Minister at Large, Christ Church, Memphis, Tennessee

"Chris Carter has a transparent love for God and people. This book is filled with humble and honest self-disclosure that leads to profound insights on faith for the dark and unfamiliar roads we travel. Through Chris' own journey one fearful night, we discover how trust and grace intersect, reminding us that God is always active in our lives, even in the most difficult storms."

Donna VanLiere, *NY Times* and *USA Today* Bestselling Author

"Written with lively passion and helpful transparency, Chris Carter takes the reader on an engaging journey into his own brokenness. All who read this book will be reminded of the life-giving hope we have in Christ, encouraged by God's strength offered to us in weakness, and affirmed that we are not alone in our suffering."

Rev. Paul Lawler, Senior Pastor, Christ Church, Memphis, Tennessee

"It was Annie Dillard who said, 'You do not have to sit outside in the dark. If, however, you want to look at the stars, you will find that darkness is required.' In Chris Carter's insightful book, *Navigating the Night*, you will discover that finding yourself in a dark place isn't always bad. In fact, the darkness will give you a focus on your relationship with God that you can't get any other way. Read slowly these warm and witty yet thought provoking reflections. In doing so, you will comfort, console, and fortify your faith."

Dr. Richard Hipps, Pastor Emeritus, Trinity Baptist Church, Cordova, Tennessee

"Pastor Chris Carter has a rare gift - honesty that shows how much he cares for others. Teddy Roosevelt once said, 'People do not care how much you know until they know how much you care.' Jesus cared enough to show his unbelieving disciples the scars in his hands and feet after his death and resurrection. After showing his scars, Christ opened their minds to help them understand and believe again (Luke 24:38-45). Pastor Chris, like Jesus, is empathic and dares to show us his scars. Someone explained the difference between sympathy and empathy. Sympathy feels our pain when we are in a pit. Empathy gets in the pit with us and helps us to climb out. Pastor Chris empathy helps us to lay aside the weight and sins that trouble us and to get out of our pit of darkness and despair."

Rev. Lonnie Royal, Sr., Retired Pastor and Hospital Chaplain

"As I write this recommendation for my former pastor Chris Carter's new book *Navigating the Night,* the darkest day of the year is just a week away, and again I'm reminded of why I love warm, sunlit days so much better than cold, dark nights. I'm also reminded that, especially these days, there are many people who are walking through times of emotional and spiritual darkness. Brother Chris shows us all how to find healing and hope in dark times. *Navigating the Night* is written with sensitivity, thorough knowledge of scripture, and a lively faith in God's loving, restorative power in times when darkness seems to be in control. I'm so glad I have this treasure of a book."

Bob Sennett, Retired Editor-in-Chief, Thomas Nelson Bibles

"I have known Chris Carter for ten years and am constantly encouraged by his biblical teaching and leadership. He has written this book the way he teaches and preaches – with deep humility, spiritual wisdom, inspiring insight, and regular humor."

Randy Wade, Retired Business Executive

"I have often heard 'never trust a skinny cook,' and I would take that a step further and say, 'don't trust someone who writes about *Navigating the Night* who does not have a history of doing so.' I have known Chris as a friend, brother, pastor, counselor, and teacher for almost five decades. Chris knows what he is writing about! In a world experiencing a mental health crisis that includes increasing statistics of people who die by suicide, this book couldn't come at a better time in history. God's direction and Chris's experience are an important reminder...Don't quit. Share this book with all who are hurting...that would instantly make this a best seller as we are all *Navigating the Night*, but all are not as willing as Chris to bring it into the light."

Rev. Anita Pringle, LPC-MHSP, Clinical Director, The Refuge Center for Counseling, Franklin, Tennessee

"As a Christian Family Therapist, one of my mottos is, '*If we cannot find Jesus in the storms of life, He surely cannot be found in the sunshine of life.*' Storms are characterized by strong winds of adversity, torrential rains for gossip, the closed slammed doors of rejection, the emotional fingerprint of abuse, and the thick clouds of hate, anger, and unforgiveness.

Like Peter walking to Jesus on the water, when we take our eyes off Him, we find our entire being engulfed by the storm. Chris Carter, in this book, has constructed a map reflective of the storms in your personal life through his experiences that mirror your life story in so many ways.

There is one significant difference. He has employed the military theme of "No person left behind." In doing so, you get the sense that he is right in your story. You will mysteriously sense his navigating you out of your storm using experiences, stories, and scripture. In doing so, you will find yourself on a path that will expose you to a sense of a resurrection from the storms to God's sunshine of hope, godly warmth, and a heavenly victory.

After completing the first chapter, you, too, will sense a compulsion to finish this masterpiece of literature to the very end."

Dr. Zawdie Abiade, President of Bridge Talk

"Brother Chris has written a book that reveals a clear message of the power of God to heal the human spirit. Modern Psychiatric Medicine and Psychology promotes humanistic concepts to explain human suffering and offers ideas for man to save himself. He has woven storytelling, personal experience, scripture, quotes from ancient and modern authors, and songs that will speak to everyone about the love of Jesus for all mankind. The Reflections sections at the end of each chapter are thought-provoking and challenge us to think deeply, meditate on our core beliefs, and open our feelings to the Holy Spirit.

He covers most every form of emotional problems- disease, illness, personality problems, traumatic life events, and motivated addiction behavior. He encourages us to use the tools of faith, laughter, praise, thanksgiving, surrender, rest, practice, and patience. The Holy Spirit touched me in a special way as I thought of how this text could help suffering people.

This book can be used personally or in a group setting. It is essential that people hear the truth from God about human suffering. This book fulfills our need to hear God's truth and help us reject Satan's lies."

Paul B Hill, MD, Assistant Professor of Psychiatry, University of Tennessee Health Sciences Center Memphis

Navigating the Night
Living by Faith & Finding Hope in Dark Times

"Let him who walks in the dark, who has no light, trust in the name of the Lord and rely on his God" (Isaiah 50:10).

Chris Carter

Copyright © 2023 Chris Carter

This book has been published in partnership with Birdsong Innovations (www.birdsonginnovations.com).

All Scripture quotations, unless otherwise indicated, are taken from the Holy Bible, New International Version®, NIV®. Copyright ©1973, 1978, 1984, 2011 by Biblica, Inc.™ Used by permission of Zondervan. All rights reserved worldwide. www.zondervan.com The "NIV" and "New International Version" are trademarks registered in the United States Patent and Trademark Office by Biblica, Inc.™

Table of Contents

Dedication..9

Acknowledgments..11

Preface..13

Chapter 1: Plunged into Darkness.............................15

Chapter 2: Struggling to See.....................................33

Chapter 3: Creeping Along..51

Chapter 4: Unfamiliar Roads.....................................63

Chapter 5: Navigational Means of Grace...................73

Chapter 6: Stay on Board..97

Chapter 7: Next Steps...115

Night Light Devotions..119

Night Light Devotion: God with Us...........................121

Night Light Devotion: Sunshine on My Shoulders.....123

Night Light Devotion: Waiting in Prayer....................125

Night Light Devotion: Bright Lights...........................127

Night Light Devotion: Eternal Light...........................129

Night Light Devotion: An Honest Fellowship.............131

Night Light Devotion: In the Hands of the Father......133

About the Author...135

Dedication

This book is dedicated to the following persons who continue to inspire me to live by faith and find hope in Christ as they have faithfully navigated their own nights.

To Chad Carter, my younger brother, who experienced the agony of divorce after thirty-two years of marriage. I thank you, Chad, for keeping your eyes on Jesus and continuing to be a free sample of God's love to others, including me. Remember that what often looks and feels like the end is but a new beginning. May God restore you!

To Chase Munden, my cousin by marriage who lost his father at twelve years of age in an accident and his mother at seventeen to unknown causes. Thank you, Chase, for looking to the Lord through it all and becoming one of the finest young men I know.

To Jim and Kim Birdwell, my friends, who have tenderly cared for their son, Zander, for twenty-eight years continuing to believe for the manifestation of his healing. Through little sleep and many battles, you continue to believe. I believe with you! May God give you strength and honor your faithfulness!

To Mike and Amy Feehan, my friends, who have kept the faith after their son, Michael, took his own life. You are exceptional parents and have been a light to many who face their own dark nights. On days when life feels too much, may God keep carrying and comforting you until you see your son again!

To Patrick and Ginger Haynes, my friends, who prayerfully

and patiently waited almost a decade for their beloved Abby to arrive while Ginger underwent cancer treatments that she is still experiencing. Your faith and joy shine brightly that our Father in heaven be praised!

May God keep your lamps burning and turn your darkness into light!

Acknowledgements

I am blessed to be surrounded by family and friends who encourage me. Thank you all for the gift of your presence in my life.

To Tonya, my wife and best friend. You are beautiful beyond description, compassionate, and full of wisdom. You light up my life!

To Brady, Connor, and Eli, our three sons. You bring me joy and laughter. Being your dad restores my soul!

To Charles and Wilma Carter, my parents, who have a living faith, loving hearts, and a robust desire to serve the Lord. You are high wattage disciples! I honor, respect, and love you!

Chuck, my older brother, and his wife Melanie, two dear loved ones who have overcome a lot to shine for Him. So proud of you!

To Lanny and Sherri Munden, my in-laws, Ty and Colt, my brothers-in-law, Ashlee and Sandy, my sisters-in-law, and all my Carter and Munden nephews and nieces: Camein, Joseph, Stephen, Stetson, Colt, Kathryn, Natalie, Laynie, Lyric, and Leddy. I love doing life together!

To Dr. Zawdie Abiade, affectionately known as "Pastor" or "Doc," thank you for being my friend, pastor, therapist, mentor, and cheerleader, for always shining brightly and reminding me of who I am in Christ when I forget. You are so loved and appreciated!

To Dr. Ben Birdsong, my editor, whose careful and encouraging help has made this book possible. I thank God for intersecting our paths.

To Pastor Mike Weaver, my friend for a decade. Thank you for always being there! We have laughed and cried together. It's a joy serving with you at Christ Church.

To Pastor Paul Lawler, Senior Pastor at Christ Church Memphis, and my friend, who has given me a place in his heart with full support and connected me to Dr. Birdsong. Thank you for leading us in such a God-honoring way.

To Dr. Maxie Dunnam, Pastor Emeritus at Christ Church Memphis, who has encouraged me again and again in ministry the past eleven years.

To so many special friends at Christ Church Memphis who have nurtured and loved me and my family beyond our imagination. There are too many to mention without leaving someone out.

Preface

Dear Reader,

No matter who you are, dark times will come. They certainly have come into my life. I am sure that you will also have some midnights in your life. Some of you may be in one now. In my heart, I don't consider myself as much of a writer as an encourager. I have a compassionate desire to pass on to you some of the ways the Lord has encouraged me when the pilot light of my own soul has flickered low. At times, I feared it had been extinguished altogether.

I offer thanks for the sacred privilege of being a fellow struggler and a frequent overcomer by God's grace. I never tire of the miracle of experiencing the flame of faith within rise again! I write this small book knowing that the faith and hope I pray to ignite in you must first burn within myself. May the Lord have mercy on us both!

You will unmistakably notice in the following pages a blend of sources and stories that represent my life, which is a melting pot between the academy and the farm – the city and the country. My father's family tree was filled with city slickers, and my mother's with country folks. Both are dear to my heart and part of God's shaping design for my life. I echo Alfred Tennyson's sentiment that *"I am part of all that I have met.*[1]*"*

As we journey together, may you experience a fresh revelation of His committed heart of love toward you. May you regain the confidence that you might have lost in dark times, and may He encourage your faith in His eternal Word and empowering Holy Spirit. The Word and Spirit

---

[1] Alfred Lord Tennyson. *Ulysses*. Line 18. Accessed from http://www.poetryfoundation.org.

working together will help you overcome your most painful circumstances and desperate feelings.

Be encouraged:

"You, O Lord, keep my lamp burning; my God turns my darkness into light" (Psalm 18:28).

"The light shines in the darkness, and the darkness has not overcome it" (John 1:5).

Warmly yours,

Chris

Chapter 1
Plunged into Darkness

I will never forget the night of February 15, 2003. Dark clouds hovered low until the rain turned into ice and snow. In the early evening, around 5:30 p.m., I left a church planting meeting near Nashville, Tennessee, headed for home in Wilmore, Kentucky, where I was in a doctoral fellowship at Asbury Theological Seminary. I was leaving Music City and headed for the Holy City! **I am learning that the road to holiness often passes through hardship first. And sometimes, we can lose our song along the way.** I felt a sense of urgency to get home because our class was scheduled to fly out of Lexington at 5 a.m. the next morning to attend a conference in sunny Arizona.

The further I got out of Nashville, the worse the storm became. Before I knew it, I had been plunged into darkness. It became a night of fright – heart-pounding, bone-chilling fright. Ice and snow covered the interstate. The windshield of my little 5-speed Volkswagen Jetta was buried underneath layers of wintry mix, and my wipers were frozen to the window. Eighteen wheelers were turned over or on their sides in the medians, and abandoned cars lined the roadsides. The interstate was slick and slippery, like an ice-skating rink. My car often slid sideways like a sled and had to be straightened up again. My arms instinctively gripped the steering wheel so tightly for survival that they were numb. Although there was no feeling in my arms, I had a gigantic, gnarled knot in my stomach.

I couldn't help but wonder, *"Will I make it home? Will I ever see my wife and son again?"* It's hard to imagine now, but at that time, I didn't have a cell phone to call to tell them of my plight or hear the comfort of their voices. The only call I could make was to God. I prayed, *"Lord, help me navigate the night."* All I could do, in the words of Jeremiah, was to *"cry out in the night...and pour my heart out in the presence of the Lord"* (Lamentations 2:19). *"God's line is never too busy to hear our call!"* I don't know who first wrote or spoke these words of comfort that rose within my heart that night, but I was counting on it!

"In my distress I called to the Lord; I cried to my God for help. From His temple He heard my voice; my cry came before Him, into His ears." - Psalm 18:6

I invite you, in your mind's eye, to join me in the front seat of my Volkswagen as a passenger as together we navigate the night. Our trip will represent our mutual journey to live by faith and find hope in our dark times.

When you came to the Lord, you may have thought you were done with darkness forever. No more traveling in the dark. Our Lord has indeed called His people *"out of darkness and into His wonderful light"* (1 Peter 2:9). But the Scripture is full of night images, everything from abandonment, betrayal, depression, disillusionment, doubt, failure, grief, imprisonment, loneliness, loss, rejection, sinfulness, suffering, trials, tribulations, and many more night intruders. The night falls upon us all and represents our continued struggle with the human condition in a broken, fallen world. We are no longer of the dark, for we have become children of the light in Jesus Christ (2 Corinthians 4:6, Ephesians 5:8), but we battle with the dark. The darkness is not in us but outside of us and seeks to stifle our faith and clobber our hope and joy. **And darkness can hover so low that we can even forget we are children of the light.**

That night, I was at an impasse – a difficult situation with no apparent way out. The ordeal caused me to reflect upon my life. **Many of my days have felt like night to me.** From a young age, from as far back as I can remember, I have battled the giants of anxiety and depression along with my top-most intimidating giant of OCD (obsessive compulsive disorder), a form of mental illness. I have enough trouble penning these words for my own eyes to read, but I am horrified to think that others might know this about me. Although I know this is a true and painful part of my story, it is hard for me to expose it. I weep to think that I still care far too much about what others think of me. But there is freedom in naming our giants. **I am learning that the road to healing often passes through confession. Sometimes, we can find our song again along the way.**

Confession is God's gracious way of helping us tell the truth to ourselves and about ourselves. It frees us from our great vulnerabilities to deception and pretense. It is also part of the testing and fine-tuning of our faith that makes us more genuine, humble, and dependent on God. **Confession lets the light in!** We must not fear that our lives can feel like a mixture of sunshine and darkness because *"the darkness shall not hide us from Him...the darkness and the light are both alike to Him,"* and *"He turns our darkness into light"* (Psalm 139:12, Psalm 18:28b). **My only goal now when darkness comes is to throw the door of my heart wide open to Him so that He can light the night.**

"If we claim to have fellowship with Him yet walk in the darkness, we lie and do not live by the truth...if we claim to be without sin, we deceive ourselves and the truth is not in us." - 1 John 1:6, 8

There are many varieties of OCD. People with Obsessive Compulsive Disorder have persistent unwanted thoughts (obsessions), and they attempt to deal with these unwanted thoughts through repetitive behaviors (compulsions). I have exhausted myself by the repetition of chronic compulsions such as:

- making sure that lids on jars are closed by excessive tightening
- making sure that doors are closed by repeatedly shutting them
- making sure that lights are truly off by flipping the switch again and again
- making sure that my back pants pocket is buttoned by feeling it over and over
- making sure my car is locked by pushing the fob key so I can hear it beep one more time
- clicking and re-clicking the save icon to make sure I don't lose anything
- reading and rereading something over and over
- arranging and rearranging things in a certain way
- cleaning or washing something until it disappears

All these repetitive rituals are about making sure – a search for assurance. As tiring as some of these rituals can be, the worst and most specific nuance of OCD I battle is religious scrupulosity, which has to do with obsessing about my relationship with God to make sure or reassure myself I am okay spiritually. For years, I endlessly rehearsed the plan of salvation in a loop-like fashion, ensuring that I had covered all the bases and had believed enough. Some common symptoms of scrupulosity are an oversensitive conscience, nagging perfectionism, intolerance of uncertainty, and a sense of over-responsibility. I want to illustrate my struggle through a story that makes me laugh. **I am learning that laughter has the power to set the captives free. I often pray that God will grant me the gift of laughing at my neurotic self.** You should try it, too – laughter is an invitation to let God into our pain. Those who don't laugh won't last!

"For the joy of the Lord is your strength." - Nehemiah 8:10

"A cheerful heart is good medicine, but a crushed spirit dries up the bones" - Proverbs 17:22

The story of three guys applying for the same job with the telephone company best describes my irrational imbalance. All three men happened to show up simultaneously to fill out their applications, so the hiring manager decided to make a deal with them. The one who could put up the most telephone poles for the day would get the job. They all went out to work hard. At the end of the day, they reported their progress. The first guy reported having put up 28 poles, to which the hiring manager expressed his approval. The second guy reported having put up 26 poles, to which the hiring manager again was impressed. The third guy came home looking totally exhausted – not a dry thread on him. He reported having put up three poles. The hiring manager looked slightly surprised and disappointed and expressed his concern by reporting the success of the first two. He said, *"They put up 28 and 26 poles – how come you put up so few?"* The third man said, **"Yeah, but did you see how much of those poles they left sticking out of the ground?"** I am the third guy for sure. Over-kill best describes my compulsive behavior.

I wish trying harder dispelled fear, but it doesn't. Usually, it leads to a heightened sense of alienating darkness which makes me feel increasingly disconnected from God, from myself, and even from reality. When I am in a cycle of escalating scrupulosity, nothing seems real or makes sense, and yet I find myself relentlessly striving to make sense of it all.

I take comfort in knowing that when things don't make sense to us, they always make sense to God (Isaiah 55:8-9). He alone understands our craziness and can restore us to His way of seeing things.

Proverbs 3:5 is a frequent go-to verse that cuts through my wrestling and realigns my heart with rest: *"Trust in the*

Lord with all your heart and lean not on your own understanding..."

My frequent over-striving is a form of control. I overwork, overthink, over-feel, over-rehearse, over-press, over-try, and end up OVER EXHAUSTED. **The road to freedom must also pass through the surrender of control.** Control is our enemy; surrender is our friend. *"I Surrender All"* has become the anthem of my soul. I will sing it until striving becomes abiding and stressing becomes resting.

All to Jesus, I surrender,
All to Him I freely give.
I will ever love and trust Him,
In His presence daily live.
I surrender all, I surrender all,
All to Thee, my blessed Savior,
I surrender all.

Sometimes, this song is more anguish than anthem. Scrupulosity has been called the disease of doubt. This seems a complete contradiction to my pastoral vocation and, more importantly, to my identity as a child of God and to whom I want to be. I often pray, *"Lord, make me a man of faith. I want to love and trust YOU without boundaries or limits."* I believe He is pleased with my desire even when I fall far short. I find encouragement in the words of C.S. Lewis: *"If only the will to walk is really present (within us), God is pleased even with our stumbles."*[2]

"So we make it our goal to please Him..."
-2 Corinthians 5:9

With the passing of time, the Lord is revealing to me that He loves all of me, not just parts of me. This is true for you too! He died for all our sins, weaknesses,

---

[2] "C. S. Lewis Quotes." *Good Reads.* Accessed from http://www.goodreads.com.

neuroses, and for all of what we call "ourselves." *"There is no pit so deep, that God's love is not deeper still,"* [3] including the great pit of self. The pit becomes powerless when we keep nothing of ourselves from Him.

"He lifted me out of the slimy pit, out of the mud and mire; He set my feet on a rock and gave me a firm place to stand." - Psalm 40:2

"Through our failures and weaknesses, we truly learn that God's love is endless." [4]

Fellow strugglers of scrupulosity wrestle with lies their minds shout at them. **Even though there is not much light at night, it seems there are many voices.** Old Testament scholar Walter Brueggeman says, *"There are many voices in the night, not all of them noble – some ignoble."* [5] These unworthy, dishonorable, despicable voices yell insults and lies all night long. You may recognize the sound of a very bad choir in your own head. This choir knows nothing of making beautiful music but only misery. This choir always hits the wrong notes. Many know the reality that Anne LaMott describes when she writes, *"My mind is like a bad neighborhood that I don't like to go into alone."* [6] The good news is that among all the voices in the night is also the voice of a loving and holy Father who alone can uproot and replace this bad choir with heavenly sounds.

"Among them (the voices in the night), is the voice of the holy God who plucks up and tears down what we have

---

[3] Pam Roswell Moore. *Life Lessons from the Hiding Place: Discovering the Heart of Corrie Ten Boom* (Grand Rapids: Chosen Books, 2012), 18.
[4] Bernard Bangley. *Nearer to the Heart of God: Daily Readings with the Christian Mystics* (Brewster: Paraclete Press, 2005), 103.
[5] Walter Brueggemann. "The Power of Dreams in the Bible," *The Christian Century*, June 28, 2005: 28-31.
[6] Anne Lamott. *Operating Instructions: A Journal of My Son's First Year* (New York, Anchor, 2005), 73.

trusted, who plants and builds what we cannot even imagine...the community of faith has known – and trusted – from the outset that there is something outside our controlled management of reality which must be heeded. Sometimes, that something turns out to be a miracle of new life."[7]

Scrupulosity is paralyzing, blocking a struggler's ability to receive the love of God, and results in an endless, fruitless battle of the mind. The harder my mind works to muzzle the voices, the louder they get. The most difficult yet most helpful thing is to ignore the voices – to refuse them attention and starve them to death. The compulsion to answer or argue with them is the beginning of a losing battle. In recent years, **I have discovered that every time I resist the ritual of response to these accusing voices is an act of faith.** I pray for persistence in my resistance until the voices of accusation have no audience.

The night not only has many voices but many faces. I am not sure which face of night is staring you down right now or what taunting giant in the night has caused you to feel disconnected from God and even yourself, but I want to encourage you. **Though night has many faces, every face and expression of the night can be overcome by God's grace.** Like Paul, who wrestled with what Scripture calls *"a thorn in the flesh,"* I am slowly understanding that God's grace is sufficient for every condemning voice and every unwelcome night intruder. What God shares with Paul also belongs to us as beloved children of God: *"My grace is sufficient for you, for my power is made perfect in weakness"* (2 Corinthians 12:9). Our weaknesses can become the handles God uses to get a hold of our lives and to reveal His love in deeper ways.

We can go into His presence in our desperation and call out for the miracle of His love. He may not zap us every time,

---

[7] J. Brent Bill. *Sacred Compass: The Way of Spiritual Discernment* (Brewster: Paraclete Press, 2008), 35.

but He finds a way to wrap us in His sustaining love when we cry out to Him.

"Let us approach the throne of grace with confidence, so that we may receive mercy and find grace to help us in our time of need." - Hebrews 4:16

Have you ever found yourself at an impasse? Perhaps a painful relationship, a job breaking you in half, an addiction, a loss, a failure, has taken you into a dark place beyond your strength and a fight with enemies and obstacles? When we find ourselves navigating the night through impasses in our lives, it is a common temptation to spend most of our time looking for bypasses, overpasses, or underpasses, any way out when the most important voice we need to hear is God's Word passed down – "Trust Me!" This word to trust is God's Word for every generation of His true followers who find themselves navigating the night. **The way out for God's people is most often the way through.**

"God didn't remove the Red Sea but parted it. Sometimes God doesn't remove our problems, but always makes a way through them."[8]

If God chooses not to remove the problem, He will use the problem to improve us!

There are seasons in our lives when we find ourselves involuntarily enrolled in the University of Adversity, where we learn the most valuable lesson: **Sometimes, God permits darkness to come for His improving purposes.** Saint John of the Cross, a 16th-century Spanish poet and mystic, often wrote about "The Dark Night of the Soul." This strong metaphor represents God's process to

---

[8]"Smith Wigglesworth and Other Generals of God." Accessed from http://www.facebook.com.

bring us into greater union with Himself. He uses these dark times to help us detach from things of this world so that we might attach more fully to Him. **There are some things we must get unhooked from to get hooked to Jesus more deeply.** Jesus, Himself told His disciples, referring to the prince of this world: *"he has no hold on Me"* (John 14:30). I pray the same for every follower of Jesus.

Over the years, Romans 8:28 has been like a soft pillow for my tired heart, especially related to OCD. I am not exactly sure how I got wired like I am, but I am thankful for the assurance Paul offers. As children of God, we live not by chance but under God's care. He writes, *"And we know that God causes all things to work together for good to those who love Him, to those who are called according to His purpose."* The phrase *"to work together"* comes from a word that means *"companions in labor."* God causes contrary circumstances and situations that, on the surface, appear to be fighting against us to become partners pulling together for His purposes. He uses the very things that threaten to destroy us or cause us to fall apart to transform us or work in our favor. I am glad He says "all things," too. That must include OCD. I believe it must include all things, even the circumstances we face that God did not intend. **God uses our trials and tribulations to work for us, not against us** for His ultimate purpose of conforming us *"to the likeness (character) of His Son"* (Romans 8:29).

One Sunday morning at a small southern church, the new pastor called on one of the older men to lead in the opening prayer. The man stood, bowed his head, and prayed, *"Lord, I hate buttermilk."*

The pastor opened one eye and wondered where this man's prayer was going. The older man continued, *"Lord, I hate lard."* Now the pastor was perplexed. The man continued, *"Lord, I ain't too crazy about plain flour either. But after you mix'em all together and bake'em in a hot oven, I just love biscuits."*

The old man prayed: *"Lord, help us to realize when life gets hard, when things come up that we don't like or understand, that we need to wait and see what You're making. After you get through mixing and baking, it'll probably be something even better than biscuits. Amen."*

There are many testimonies of the night where God used contrary circumstances for His glory and the good of His people. If you are navigating the night, you find yourself in good company. Remember, the voices and faces of the night are many and different for each of us, but we can trust the One who died for us and was raised from the dead for us and can find hope in Him. He will bring us through!

A dear friend with many years of experience navigating the night put his hand on my shoulder during a dark time and said with great encouragement, *"Brother Chris, God will pull you through if you can stand the pull!"* Since then, I often pray, *"Lord, help me go with Your pull, not against it."*

Nancie Carmichael shares the time in her late thirties when her physical and emotional health was broken. She became consumed with the thought of no longer wanting to live. She writes: *"Nothing is turning out the way I thought it would, and life seemed too much to bear...I felt a glob of unworthiness that I could not tie down to any concrete sins I was guilty of. What I needed more than pardon was a sense that God accepted me, owned me, held me, affirmed me, and would never let me go even if he was not too impressed with what he had on his hands."* [9]

King David cried out for mercy when he was feeling the pain of his troubled life: *"You have put me in the lowest pit, in the darkest depths"* (Psalm 88:6).

Elijah, the seemingly invincible, powerful prophet who had

---

[9] John Maxwell, Tommy Barnett, Jill Briscoe, and Nancie Carmichael. *The Desert Experience: Personal Reflections on Finding God's Presence and Promise in Hard Times* (Nashville: Thomas Nelson Publishers, 2001), 59.

such a Spirit-filled ministry under such a great anointing, said, *"I have had enough; take my life"* (1 Kings 19:4).

And John Bunyan, a faithful street preacher, once wrote: *"My soul was like a broken vessel. It was driven by the winds. It was tossed headlong into despair. It was shattered to pieces on the rocks...Greatly depressed, I walked to a neighboring town and sat down on a park bench. I sat still and thought about all of this for a long time. When I looked around, it seemed that the stones in the streets and the tiles on the houses were shunning me. I thought the sun gave its light begrudgingly. I felt unwelcomed in this world. Everyone else seemed much happier than I."* [10]

Abraham Lincoln suffered two major breakdowns. His law partner and good friend, William Herndon, said of Lincoln that *"His melancholy dripped from him as he walked."* [11]

Elie Wiesel, a Holocaust survivor, writes of eight words that changed his life forever: *"Men to the left! Women to the right!"* As a little boy, he remembers dropping the hands of his mother and sister and watching them disappear into the distance as he walked on with his father into the longest night of his life. The circumstances he saw and experienced caused him to write: *"Never shall I forget that nocturnal silence which deprived me, for all eternity, of the desire to live. Never shall I forget those moments which murdered my God and my soul and turned my dreams to dust. Never shall I forget these things, even if I am condemned to live as long as God Himself. Never."* [12]

Scripture says, *"From the sixth hour until the ninth hour darkness came over all the land. About the ninth hour Jesus cried out in a loud voice, 'My God, My God, why have you forsaken me?'"* (Matthew 27:46).

---

[10] Bernard Bangley. *Nearer to the Heart of God: Daily Readings with the Christian Mystics* (Brewster: Paraclete Press, 2005), 35.
[11] Joshua Wolf Shenk. *The Atlantic.* October 2005 Issue.
[12] Elie Wiesel. *The Night Trilogy #1: Night.* (New York: Bantam, 1982).

Notice in each of these persons an honest and desperate faith. *"There is no attempt in Scripture to whitewash the anguish of God's people when they undergo suffering...They argue with God, they complain to God, they weep before God. Theirs is not a faith that leads to dry-eyed stoicism, but to a faith so robust it wrestles with God."* [13] This kind of faith cries out to God and holds on to God not just as **though** our lives depend on Him, but **because** our lives depend on Him.

"It just rains all the time" is an old expression to describe hard times. Often the seasons of the soul mirror the seasons and cycles of nature. Darkness can hover so low that it can threaten to put out our light. Perhaps you are asking if your night will ever pass and will the sun ever shine again?
Be encouraged.

In those moments when we feel like a glob of unworthiness, the Lord helps us receive the gift of being made worthy before we feel worthy. He declares us to be worthy and says that in Christ Jesus, there is no condemnation nor separation from His love (Romans 8:1, 37-39). This is a gigantic gift in a world where proving ourselves is everything. When we struggle with that awful, aching sense of never being enough, the Lord reminds us that it is His love and mercy through Christ that declares us worthy, not our performance (Ephesians 2:4-9).

The Lord rescued David from the pit. He brought Him through! And we are still talking about this great Shepherd-King today, from whose family tree our Savior comes.

An angel touched Elijah, spoke God's truth to him, prepared a meal for him, ordered him to rest, and gave him instructions where he experienced both God's Presence

---

[13] D.A. Carson. *How Long, O Lord?: Reflections on Suffering and Evil* (Grand Rapids: Baker Academic, 2006), 63-82.

and heard His voice again.

John Bunyan had every reason to be depressed and discouraged. He was thrown into prison for preaching the gospel on the streets, but a prisoner he was not. On the back of milk bottle stops, he wrote *Pilgrim's Progress*, the number two best seller in history next to the Bible. Through his character, young Christian, Bunyan deposits faith and hope in the hearts of night navigators by reminding them that they are not alone (Isaiah 43:1-7). God is with them in their struggles which pale in comparison to the glory that awaits them (Romans 8:18). We must persevere and cheer for one another until the very end.

Lincoln became the sixteenth President of the United States of America, considered by many historians to be one of the greatest Presidents ever. He was God's man in issuing the Emancipation Proclamation. "Set my people free" was not only Moses' message but also Lincoln's.

Elie Wiesel survived the Holocaust, one of the most horrific nights in human history, and became a champion for peace and kindness among people.

Jesus was raised from the dead and delivered from the tomb's darkness, never to experience forsakenness from His Father again. He also promises us that a day is coming when *"He will wipe every tear from our eyes. There will be no more death or mourning or crying or pain, for the old order of things will pass away"* and *"all things will be made new"* (Revelation 21:4-5).

We have a magnet of a little girl on our refrigerator. She is standing in the rain clad in soggy sneakers and a drenched cotton dress, with her hands lifted up to heaven and a smile on her face. The caption below reads:

"Then, when it seems we will never smile again, life comes back!"

Little Orphan Annie sang, *"The sun will come out tomorrow!"* Lord, let it be so!

"*In every midnight, there is a budding morrow.*" [14]

---

[14] John Keats. "To Homer."

Questions for Thought And Discussion

Chapter 1 – Plunged into Darkness

Perhaps you have found yourself plunged into darkness or feeling like the pilot light of your soul is flickering low.

1. In this present moment, what are you trusting God to bring you through? Name it.

Remember, there is healing and restoration in confession. It lets the light in.

2. Have you shared with God and a few others in detail the pain of your situation? If not, why?

3. Have you ever been told by someone that you have some control issues? Do you think there is any truth to this? What do you think God wants you to do with these control issues?

4. Have you accepted the truth that God loves all of you? Is there any part of you that you have trouble believing God loves?

5. Name one thing in chapter 1 that you find encouraging? Or name one thing in the chapter that you will always remember?

6. Whose story can you most identify with out of the people I mentioned:
   a. Chris and his struggle with OCD
   b. Nancie Carmichael
   c. King David
   d. Elijah
   e. John Bunyan
   f. Elie Wiesel
   g. Jesus
   h. Little girl with her hands lifted to heaven in the rainstorm

7. Is there anything to be learned in God's ministry of darkness?

A dear friend, Randy Wade, often asks himself two questions when dealing with an issue that seems to have no solution and is consuming his thoughts:

1) God, what can I find in this situation to praise You for?
2) Holy Spirit, what are You wanting me to learn from this tribulation?

Others might be:

3) How can I best express my love for You through what I am going through?
4) Do I have a victim mentality or am I trusting God to make me an overcomer?

What other questions might you ask?

Chapter 2
Struggling to See

"We live by faith, not by sight" (2 Corinthians 5:7).

"As it is written, 'The righteous shall live by faith'" (Habakkuk 2:4, Romans 1:17).

I penned in my journal concerning that frightful night: *"As I navigated the night, I could see little. My defroster had no melting power in the face of old man winter. It simply couldn't keep up. My side mirrors looked like clear blocks of ice protruding from the car, and my front windshield was a winter landscape continually battered by ice and snow until my wipers didn't work at all. I could see only through a single, tiny hole in the middle of the window. I had to strain my neck and tilt my head low to peer through.* **There was not much sight but just enough for the night!***"*

I was struggling to see. A few years ago, I spoke with two grand adults, Betty Shipmon and Ken Stepherson, who knew this struggle physically. These friends were well into their nineties and suffering from macular degeneration. This eye disease destroys the central portion of the retina and causes vision loss in the center of a person's field of vision. Rarely does it cause total blindness but a severe narrowing of vision. Victims can see, but only that right in front of them. Despite this difficult degeneration of physical vision, Mrs. Shipmon and Mr. Stepherson both glowed with a mighty spirit of regeneration and increasing faith in God's presence with them in their dark times.

Ann was my 97-year-old great aunt. She was a simple, country woman sporting only one tooth on the top row and wearing an old-fashioned house dress. She couldn't read or write but had a splendid personality and was full of compliments. One summer afternoon, when I was a teenager visiting Aunt Ann, she said, *"Chris, you sure are a good-looking young man."* I said, *"Aunt Ann, thank you, but you must be blind."* She said, *"I am."* We laughed together! There is nothing quite like getting a compliment about your looks from someone who can't see.

It is not only the elderly who struggle to see. Partial vision is part of the plight of the human condition. Apostle Paul is known for contrasting the partial with the complete, the now with the then. He says, *"**Now** we see but a poor reflection as in a mirror; **then** we shall see face to face. **Now** I know in part; **then** I shall know fully, even as I am fully known"* (1 Corinthians 13:12). A few verses before, Paul reminds us that *"**(now)** we know in part and we prophesy in part, but **(then)** when perfection comes, the imperfect disappears"* (13:9). In this already, but not yet time, this in-between time between earth and heaven, our knowledge, reasoning, and sight are limited. **We see partially but not perfectly.** This incomplete vision affects how we see God, ourselves, others, and life itself.

Someone said, *"Life is like watching a parade through a knot hole in the fence."* Imagine it – we would only be able to see what is passing directly in front of us at any given time, but not the full picture. We don't know everything, and we don't see everything clearly or completely, including the Lord and His plan. Faith is trusting God when we can't see or can see only very little. Sometimes Habakkuk 2:4, *"but the righteous will live by his (the believer's) faith"* is translated as *"but the righteous will live by His (God's) faithfulness."* **It is a mistake to focus on our faith rather than His faithfulness because the essence of living by faith is not our frantic activity but God's faithful activity on our behalf.**

Faith is needed now when night comes, but it won't be necessary when we get to heaven because our faith will be sight, and we will see better than ever the power of His faithfulness.

An English monk who lived in the middle of the 14th century spoke of *"the cloud of unknowing."* He used this expression to refer to the seasons and times of darkness in the lives of people of faith when their vision is cloudy or foggy. They fail to see or sense things clearly. **I have prayed so often when my days have felt like nights, and I am struggling to see for God to give me night vision!** I don't pray to see perfectly, but that I will have enough sight for the night, that I will see with my spirit and heart what can't be seen with my eyes.

"Faith is like radar which sees through the fog – it sees the reality of things at a distance that the human eye cannot see." [15]

I would like you to pause and pray for the Lord to illumine the eyes of your heart.

"I pray that the eyes of your heart may be enlightened in order that you may know the hope to which He has called you, the riches of His glorious inheritance in the saints, and His incomparably great power for you who believe." - Ephesians 1:18-19

I also pray for you: *"Lord, give my friends who are reading my story and living their stories night vision for their own nights! Help them experience You as their pillar of cloud by day to lead the way, and their pillar of fire by night to give them light!"* (Exodus 13:21).

I am learning that the more God shines on our hearts and gives them light, the stronger our awareness of darkness becomes. Jesus called the Church in Laodicea blind because they pridefully thought they could see (Revelation 3:17). They had huge blind spots and didn't even know it.

---

[15] Pam Roswell Moore. *Life Lessons from the Hiding Place: Discovering the Heart of Corrie Ten Boom* (Grand Rapids: Chosen Books, 2012), 16.

The old Jewish prayer says it best: *"Days pass and years vanish, and we walk sightless among miracles."*[16]

We all struggle with blind spots, and sometimes the Lord is gracious enough to reveal them to us. I've never laughed harder than hearing the story of a young couple who recently moved into a new neighborhood. One morning while eating breakfast, the young woman saw her neighbor hanging the wash outside on the clothesline. She said, *"That wash is not very clean...she doesn't know how to wash correctly, perhaps she needs better laundry soap."*

Her husband looked on but remained silent.

Every time her neighbor would hang her wash to dry, the young woman would make the same comments.

About one month later, the woman was surprised to see a nice clean wash on the line and said to her husband:

"Look, she has learned how to wash correctly. I wonder who taught her this."

The husband said, *"I got up early this morning and cleaned our windows."*

The same is true in life. What we see when watching others and sizing up life's events depends on the purity of the window through which we look. The more we walk in the light, the more awareness we have of the darkness and the closer our perspective is to God's. It is also true that the Holy Spirit can illumine our understanding and help us to see our blind spots and overcome them. The Holy Spirit shines God's light exposing and expelling darkness of the mind and heart.

---

[16] Susan Sparks. *Miracle on 31st Street* (Coppell, TX, 2022), 12.

"But the Counselor, the Holy Spirit...will teach you all things and will remind you of everything I have said to you." - John 14:26

At times, we are simply blind to what God is doing. We are like Jesus' disciples on the Road to Emmaus. Before they really understood that Jesus had been raised, they were navigating the night NOT SO WELL! Their hopes had been dashed – *"they had hoped that Jesus was the one who was going to redeem Israel"* (Luke 24:21). After the crucifixion, they had given up hope. They no longer believed that something good or better could lie ahead. I can picture them on the road kicking rocks and wondering in stunned confusion what in the world had happened – *"they stood still their faces downcast"* (24:17). The Message says, *"they were long-faced, like they had lost their best friend."*[17] That's the way they felt. Jesus had been taken from them. Can you relate? Has something or someone been taken from you, and you couldn't see how anything good could come out of the mess you felt?

As these two disciples continued to walk the Road to Emmaus, they *"were talking with each other about everything that had happened"* (24:14). There is an ache in them, an indescribable gut grief. It made them talk, or I should say, complain out loud. When we can't see, we talk. That's what we do in the night, isn't it? We talk things to death. We talk, talk, talk about our problems, all the bad things that have happened. In our passionate rehearsal, we usually multiply our anxiety, and we work ourselves into a fresh lather of negativity and fear.

Did you hear about the guy who blew a tire while driving through the country? He became even more distressed when he discovered there was no jack in his trunk. Looking down the dark road, he saw a distant farmhouse with a light on. It was his only option, so he started walking.

---

[17] Eugene Peterson. *The Message* (Colorado Springs: NavPress, 2002).

During his journey, he started thinking, *"What if nobody's home?"* A little later, he thought, *"What if they're home, but they don't have a jack?"* His adrenaline started pumping even more when he asked himself, *"What if they have a jack but won't let me use it?"* This private conversation in his mind escalated to the point that when he finally arrived at the house, he simply yelled at the farmer, *"You can just keep your stupid jack!"*

In my frightful night, I experienced moments of negative internal dialogue that were filled with panic and questions. What if I don't make it home? Why is this happening? How long will this last? Will I make it through? This negative dialogue is the most draining, debilitating aspect of scrupulosity when it revisits.

The heaviest burdens that we carry are the thoughts in our own heads. Do you struggle with negative self-talk when life seems TOO BIG?

"Many believers are defeated because they let their problems talk to them rather than talking to their problems about how great a loving and powerful God they have." [18]

On a Cracker Barrel Coffee Mug was printed the saying: *"I am going to try to be positive, but I know it won't work."* Though the coffee mug is humorous, it points to an important truth: we must get unhooked from negativity and self-depreciation.

Our SELF-TALK is so important. *"We all talk to ourselves. We are, each of us, our own all-day, all-talk radio stations with one devoted listener...Our thoughts have incredible power in our lives, and if our self-talk is self-defeating, we'll feel like quitting."* [19]

---

[18] D. Martin Lloyd-Jones. *Spiritual Depression: Its Causes and Cure* (Grand Rapids: Eerdmans, 1965), 21.
[19] Kyle Idleman. *Don't Give Up: Faith that Gives You Confidence to Keep Believing and Courage to Keep Going* (Grand Rapids: Baker Books, 2019), 72.

Someone wrote, *"If we talked to our friends in the same way we talked to ourselves we would not have any friends."*

When our days feel like night, we need to remember that Jesus called us friends if we do what He commands (John 15:15). He does not talk to us the way we talk to ourselves but as a true and faithful friend. We must not speak words to ourselves that are unkind and cause even more pain. We must speak His words, His truth. We must preach to ourselves the words of Jesus and pray for the faith to listen to every word of His with the intent to obey and be shaped by His Word.

As the disciples continued to walk in the disillusionment, *"Jesus Himself came up and walked along with them"* (24:15). **Jesus didn't leave them in the night; He joined them!** How many times has Jesus found us on the negative trail of defeat? No matter what we go through, God never takes His eyes off us. He joins us in the night. I once had a job working the third shift, cleaning up the floors in a blue jean factory. It was hot, dirty, and discouraging. One night while all alone in this massive warehouse while all my friends were sleeping, I heard a divine whisper, *"Chris, my son, you are not alone. I work all night too and all day."* **God works every shift, but especially the night shift.**

Zach William's album, *Rescue Story,* includes the hit song by him and Dolly Parton, entitled "There Was Jesus," which stresses Jesus' presence with us specifically during dark times:

'When the life I built came crashing to the ground
When the friends I had were nowhere to be found
I couldn't see it then, but I can see it now
There was Jesus

In the waiting, in the searching
In the healing and the hurting

*Like a blessing buried in the broken pieces
Every minute, every moment
Where I've been and where I'm going
Even when I didn't know it or couldn't see it
There was Jesus*

*On the mountain, in the valleys (There was Jesus)
In the shadows of the alleys (There was Jesus)
In the fire, in the flood (There was Jesus)
Always is and always was
No I never walk alone (Never walk alone)
You are always there!"*[20]

Psalm 121:4-7 says, *"He doesn't slumber nor sleep. He watches over us...He watches over our lives; over our coming and going both now and forevermore."* Jesus says, *"I am always with you, even to the end of the age"* (Matthew 28:20). Although God never takes His eyes off us and promises to always be with us, there are times when we don't recognize Him. Luke says, *"but the disciples were kept from recognizing Jesus"* (24:16). Our slowness in recognizing our Savior and Friend can be an act of special divine intervention. It suggests that sometimes God helps us see things more clearly, but other times He might delay our seeing something for a greater purpose UNTIL THE RIGHT TIME! The right time is God's perfect, appointed time.

It is interesting to remember that Saul's time of great light was also a time of great darkness. After his dramatic conversion experience, he continued blind until the Lord sent Ananias to pray for him, and something like scales fell from his eyes, and he could see again (Acts 9:17-19). **Sometimes our blinding results in a fresh finding of God in our lives.**

*"The stripping away of our false selves both demands and

---

[20] Zach Williams. "There Was Jesus." Track 7 on *Rescue Story*. Provident Label Group LLC. 2019.

creates a temporary darkness. It's almost as if the burning away of old patterns and the accompanying of illumination that comes from discovering the true self create light so bright that it blinds us for a while."* [21] **God is at work within us, helping us to discover our true selves in Him!**

In some awesome and miraculous sense, Christ entered our darkness when He came to earth as a human being. He willingly plunged Himself into the human condition so we could find Him or be found by Him. He still comes into our brokenness and sin, suffers with us, and weeps with us. And He even calls to us from the darkness. *"For six days the cloud covered the mountain, and on the seventh day the Lord called Moses from within the cloud...then Moses entered the cloud"* (Exodus 24:16, 18a). As God gave the Ten Commandments, *"the people remained at a distance, while Moses approached the thick darkness where God was"* (Exodus 20:21). To what end might our Lord be calling to you in the night of your life?

Jesus walks along with them to ask them about the topic of their discussion. He already knew, but I love how He tenderly pursues them to help them find Him. He does the same with us! The disciples tell Jesus what He already knew, and *"He explained to them beginning with Moses and all the Prophets what was said in all the Scriptures concerning Himself"* (Luke 24:27). Jesus turned to Scripture in the night! So should we! As He opened and shared Scripture, the disciples' hearts started burning inside them (24:32).

"As they approached the village to which they were going, Jesus acted as if He were going further (if they had not invited Him in, maybe He would have continued walking by Himself). *But they urged Him strongly, stay with us, for it is nearly evening; the day is almost over. So, He went in to*

---

[21] Sue Monk Kidd. *When the Heart Waits: Spiritual Direction for Life's Sacred Questions* (New York: Harper One, 1990), 151.

stay with them" (24:28-29).

Jesus not only joins us in our nights, but He stays with us at our invitation. In a sense, He is always with us no matter what; but in another deeper sense, He is with us most fully at our invitation, at our personal urging. So often, we expect God to bless our lives and relationships when we have not even taken the time to specifically urge and invite Him into those troubled areas and relationships by name or situation. **We must invite Jesus into the nights of our lives.** Please stop and take some time to call out to Him concerning the personal details of your life. Invite Him into every problem and relationship, and thank Him that He will make Himself known in just the right way at just the right time.

IT WAS NOW THE RIGHT TIME! *"When He was at the table with them, He took bread, gave thanks, broke it, and began to give it to them. Then their eyes were opened, and they recognized Him..."* Although He may seem hidden to us by night, we shall see Him again in His time. Our eyes will be opened, and we will recognize Him and see to what end He was working in the night.

"...and He disappeared from their sight" (24:32). Just when they see Jesus, He vanishes again. **We don't control Him. We don't get God on our own terms.** This doesn't keep us from trying, but we must remember that He chooses when we see Him and when we don't! This way, we learn to walk by faith and not by sight (2 Corinthians 5:7).

In his wonderful book *The Presence: Experiencing More of God,* Alec Rowlands makes this essential point, *"My friend, take heart: If you have been searching diligently for God's presence but haven't encountered Him yet, don't be discouraged...He will reveal Himself to you exactly when and where and how He wants to. Never before. Never because you're in the driver's seat. And always just in* time."[22]

As a teenager, I often heard our dear friend, Evangelist James Norman remind God's people: **"God sometimes seems slow, but He is never late!"**

The main thing we need to remember is to keep pursuing God, to love Him, and seek to know Him intimately and He will completely surprise us and even overwhelm us with His presence right on time.

The idea of not controlling God is a needed one for a night traveler, especially an OCD sufferer. We can work very hard to make sure outcomes are positive. Christians are not to be those who seek control but surrender control. We thank God that He is in control and are willing to give up control of our lives to His sovereign hand and good and wise heart.

As you navigate the night in your life, as you struggle to see, thank the Lord for your limitations and weaknesses. God places a special grace on those who admit their blindness and uses our humble awareness to bring us to Himself. His grace will be sufficient for your night journey, no matter what it is, for His power will be made perfect in your surrendered weakness (2 Corinthians 12:9).

It is our religious pride that we must be concerned about. Jesus once reminded a man born blind, whose eyes He miraculously opened, that He came *"into this world, so that the blind will see and those who see* (or who think they can see) *will become blind"* (John 9:39). This is not as confusing as it may first sound. It is Jesus warning that only those whose hearts are opened to Him can truly see, no matter how good their physical vision may be, or how much they think they may know (John 9:41).

---

[22] Alec Rowlands with Marcus Brotherton. *The Presence: Experiencing More of God.* (Grand Rapids: Tyndale House Publishers, 2014), 24.

Life on the family farm required whole family participation. Everybody had chores to do, including Calvin, an eight-year-old boy. Each morning before school and after school, he did his part to help the family.

In October, after the clocks had been turned back, he came home to do his chores and discovered it was already dark. His dad told him to get to it! Calvin stepped out on the front porch to make his way to the barn. While standing on the porch, he grew scared. The night was dark, and he could not see where the barn was.

He went back inside the house and told his dad how he felt. His dad was wise and said, *"You are becoming a big boy now. We trust you to carry a lantern to the barn and do your chores."* He lit the lantern and sent his son onto the porch carrying the light into the darkness.

He stood on the porch...holding up the lantern...but could not see more than a few feet in front of his face. He, for sure, couldn't see the barn across the yard. He was still scared.

He went back inside and told his dad how he felt. His dad said, *"Son, do you trust me?"* The boy said, *"Yes."* His dad said, *"Do you believe me when I told you that the barn is still out there across the yard?"* The boy said, *"Yes."* His dad said, *"Then, I want you to go back outside and take a step off the porch toward the direction of the barn.* **Take one step at a time and work toward the edge of your light**, *and I promise you the barn is still there."*

When you struggle to see, just take one step at a time, trusting Jesus. Don't try to see too far ahead of yourself. Thank God for whatever you can see and remember that life will not always be like watching a parade through a knot hole in the fence – someday, you will be lifted above the fence and see that all of life is part of God's plan.

> *"So we fix our eyes not on what is seen, but on what is unseen. For what is seen is temporary, but what is unseen is eternal." - 2 Corinthians 4:18*

I will never forget an inner-city mission trip to Pittsburgh during my junior year in high school. On this trip, I met a very special woman. Mary was a homeless woman in her eighties standing in the soup kitchen line. The edges of her gray hair were hanging down on her brow beneath the soiled scarf wrapped around her head. The wrinkles in her tanned face looked like well-traveled roads, but I sensed that the wrinkles weren't just from a hard life but from all the times she had smiled.

I could hardly believe my ears, but this high-mileage woman was singing rather than sighing. The light that shined from her countenance caused me to think of the brilliant words of Dr. Elisabeth Kubler-Ross, *"People are like stained glass windows. They sparkle and shine when the sun is out, but when the darkness sets in, their true beauty is revealed only if there is a light from within."*[23] I am confident that Jesus was the light within Mary.

After she finished singing a hymn, I shook her hand and asked how she was. With a smile spread across her face, bright as a rainbow, she said, *"I am so blessed."* She was a woman of deep and radiant joy! "How?" I thought. She must have been looking into another world, a world beyond, seeing something others could not realize.

Scripture encourages every saint to look behind the scenes. We are to look up and away from the impermanent appearances of this present world scene. We are to look to the spiritual, not the material. *"For what is seen is temporary, but what is unseen is eternal"* (2 Corinthians 4:18a). *"Since, then, you have been raised with Christ, set*

---

[23] "Elizabeth Kubler-Ross Quotes." *Good Reads.* Accessed from http://www.goodreads.com.

your hearts on things above...set your minds on things above, not on earthly things" (Colossians 3:1-2a).

When by faith, God gives us a glimpse of what's behind the scenes, we can sing rather than sigh. Paul says, *"Praise be to the God and Father of our Lord Jesus Christ, who has blessed us with every spiritual blessing in Christ"* (Ephesians 1:3). Paul couldn't have written this from a prison cell in Rome unless he had learned to look behind the scenes of present circumstances. He knew that *"our light and momentary troubles are achieving for us an eternal glory that far outweighs them all"* (2 Corinthians 4:17).

At times, we are simply blind because we are looking at the wrong things. Everybody has a focal point, something we are focused on. We can choose to be **problem-centered**, where our mental and emotional energies go towards dwelling on or fixing problems. This can happen easily because we've all got problems. I laughingly say, *"We either have a problem, are a problem, or live with a problem."* The deficiency in this way of living is that we are always either in a problem, coming out of a problem, or going into one.

We can also choose to be **project-centered**, where our mental and emotional energies go toward getting things done. We can become so task-oriented and driven that we can't rest until everything is done. The deficiency in this way of living is that everything will never be done – something will always replace it. Being problem-centered or project-centered will result in frustration, dread, or exhaustion, which all rob our hearts of joy and hope.

The best choice to make is to be **Person-centered**, where our mental and emotional energies go towards looking towards God, setting our focus and affection on Him as our loving and faithful Father who guides and provides. He enjoys us and wants us to enjoy Him.

The Psalmist says, *"I have set the Lord always before me..."* (Psalm 16:8a). He doesn't say that he always sees the Lord, feels the Lord, or experiences the Lord, but that he sets the Lord before him. He is determined to think on the Lord, to look to the Lord, to seek His Person and Presence, no matter what.

What are you looking at – problems, projects, or the Lord? The temporary or the permanent, the visible or the invisible? It's easy to become imprisoned by present circumstances and to lose heavenly vision. We must fight for sight. Take a moment to pray, *"Lord, help me see behind the scenes again."*

Prayer:

"May I see Thee more clearly,
Love Thee more dearly,
and follow Thee more nearly"

(Saint Richard of Chichester – 13th century)[24]

---

[24] Saint Richard of Chichester. Accessed from the Mary Foundation at http://www.catholicity.com.

Questions for Thought And Discussion

Chapter 2 – Struggling to See

We are only human and struggle to see the things of God perfectly (1 Corinthians 13:9-12). Although we see only partially, there are certainly times when God speaks to us to help us see better.

1. In your struggle to see, has God ever:
   a. Revealed a blind spot in your life? Shined His light on something?
   b. Given you a revelation of something that puzzled you before?
   c. Taken you into a deeper awareness of His real presence?
   d. Made you more aware of the presence of darkness in your life?

2. Have you ever prayed *"for the eyes of your heart to be enlightened?"* (Ephesians 1:18). Take a moment to do this now. Ask God to reveal to you anything He desires.

In this chapter, I include the following quotation: *"If we talk to our friends in the same way we talk to ourselves, we would not have any friends."*

3. Do you ever struggle with negative self-talk? Rate how kind your talk to yourself is on a scale from 1-10, with ten being the kindest.

4. When is the last time you remember inviting Jesus into some night of your life? Do you need to do this now? Remember that He works the night shift!

5. Is there some area of your life where you need to remember what the little boy's father told him: *"Take one step at a time and work toward the edge of your light..."*

Scripture teaches that we can choose what we focus on (2 Corinthians 4:18, Colossians 3:1-2). We can look at the temporary things or eternal, the visible or invisible, the earthly or heavenly.

6. Where are your eyes fixed right now? Where is your attention going?

Chapter 3
Creeping Along

Thank you for continuing to ride with me. I am still on the interstate in my little VW, navigating the night. My journal read, *"The ice and snow are falling fast. As the storm worsened, I crept along at 5-10 miles per hour, trying to coast as often as I could to give my tired clutch foot a break."*

I crept along...I slowed down. Often when we are in a dark time, we tend to speed up rather than slow down. We try and outrun the night! But speeding often sends us to the ditch. It's amazing how many people drive faster when the winter storm hits, but usually not for long. Beware – a crash is coming.

We like the word "go" better than the word "slow." We are card-carrying members of the cult of speed. We like keeping up better than creeping along. We like zipping more than sipping. We are addicted to moving fast – to the adrenaline of trying to save ourselves. **We would rather live by the momentum rather than by the moment.** We also fill our lives. We cram them so full that we leave little to no space for God to speak, yet we are not fulfilled. I sometimes wonder if God graciously pauses the momentum button in our lives to see if we can learn to live in the moment. I thank Him for the miracle of allowing us to feel from time to time how crammed our lives are with empty things. We often resist God's invitation to slow down in the name of responsibility, even when we are barely hanging on by a thread. Perhaps we need to thank the Lord for the conditions in our lives that He uses that require us to slow down.

That little Volkswagen could go 160 MPH, but I had to slow down to 5 MPH. **Does it frustrate you to go slower than you want to?** My wife and sons accuse me of driving too slow. They get frustrated with me and laugh that the highway patrol would think their radar is broken if they ever zeroed in on me. They think I make a snail look respectable and say the spiders in my hubcaps barely get dizzy! This is contrasted with my lovely wife, who goes so fast that my hair blows even when the windows are up!

Mother Teresa once observed that *"Everybody today seems to be in such a terrible rush, anxious for greater developments."* [25] Why is it that we think developments only occur from going faster?

If we slow down, we think nothing is happening. But this is not true.

"One sure mark of genuine spiritual growth...is a growing preference for the ordinary days of our life with God. We gradually begin to realize that it is when nothing seems to be happening that the most important things are really taking place." [26]

I want to be free from what William Faulkner once called *"the frantic steeplechase toward nothing which is the essence of worldliness everywhere."* [27] There is no need to live like we are in a steeplechase. **Remember that the essence of living by faith is not our frantic activity but God's faithful activity on our behalf.**

"I do not believe we have even begun to understand the wonderful power there is in being still. We are in such a hurry, always doing, that we are in danger of not allowing God the opportunity to work. You may be sure that God will never say to us, 'Stand still,' or 'Sit still,' or 'Be still,' unless He is going to do something. This is our problem regarding the Christian life: we want to do something to be

---

[25] Mother Teresa. *The Spiritual Life.* Accessed from http://www.slife.org.
[26] Thomas Green. *When the Well Runs Dry: Prayer Beyond the Beginnings* (Notre Dame: Ave Marie Press, 1979), 24.
[27] Robert Inchausti, ed. *New Seeds Pocket Classics: The Pocket Thomas Merton.* (Boston: New Seeds, 2005), 102.

Christians, instead of allowing Him to work in us..."²⁸

"Think of how still you stand when your picture is taken, as the photographer captures your likeness on film. God has one eternal purpose for us: that we should be 'conformed to the likeness of His Son' (Romans 8:29). *But in order for that to happen, we must stand still. We hear so much today about being active, but maybe we need to learn what it means to be quiet."*²⁹

Elijah was one of God's special servants who had forgotten this even after many powerful victories when God did the impossible. Elijah was a man of great courage, faith, and speed. He was used to living by the momentum rather than by the moment. He outran King Ahab's chariot when the power of the Lord came upon him. He was an original *Chariots of Fire* member.

He appeared to be afraid of nothing – not afraid to be called a troublemaker by King Ahab for challenging Israel's disobedience and idolatry, not afraid to tell the king that a drought was on the way, not afraid to tell the widow of Zarephath not to be afraid in her own dark night, not afraid to call out to God when the widow's son was so sick he could have died (yet he lived), not afraid to duel with 450 prophets of Baal to prove that Yahweh was the only true God...not afraid of anything EXCEPT a woman with a wagging tongue who was breathing murderous threats. **Everybody has a breaking point!** Elijah was at his. You may be at yours?

He had been in the heat of the battle for a long time. He was battle weary and had become blind to his need to slow down. He had become discouraged by Israel's disobedience and tired of being the only faithful one left, he thought. Self-pity had set in. Self-pity loves to exercise squatter's rights and make itself at home. It had become very at

---

[28] L.B. Cowman, *Streams in the Desert* (Chump Change Publishers, 1925), 61.
[29] L.B. Cowman, *Streams in the Desert* (Chump Change Publishers, 1925), 62.

home in Elijah. He had become lonely, hiding out with only ravens for three years. **It's not always the weight of our burdens that gets us but how long we carry them.** Elijah's confidence in God's triumphal power was waning, and he was withdrawing from the conflict. He was depressed and fearful. He became afraid after Jezebel threatened his life. Scripture says, *"Elijah was afraid and ran for his life"* (1 Kings 19:3). Out of fear, he ran into the desert, sat down under a tree, and prayed to die (19:4).

Elijah was so exhausted that *"he lay down under the tree and fell asleep"* (19:5). It sounds like he was forced to slow down! But God doesn't leave him in his dark night; He joins him and revives him.

God sent an angel to touch him while he was asleep. *"He gives His angels charge concerning us, to guard us in all our ways"* (Psalm 91:11). The angel roused Elijah after he slept for a while and encouraged him to get up and eat some bread the angel baked over hot coals and drink from a jar of water prepared for him. Scripture says, *"He ate and drank and then lay down again"* (19:6). **There is only one thing better than a nap – and that's two naps!** Sometimes taking a nap is the most spiritual thing we can do. Then we learn that the angel touched Elijah a second time. **There is only one thing better than getting touched by an angel once – and that's getting touched again!** Lord, touch your people once again. We cannot make it without your fresh touch.

Millions of saints above and below who know the reality of His life-restoring touch rave about it and crave it still. Those who have experienced it love to sing together the beautiful words of *He Touched Me*:

"Shackled by a heavy burden
'Neath a load of guilt and shame
Then the hand of Jesus touched me
And now I am no longer the same

*He touched me, oh, He touched me
And oh, the joy that floods my soul
Something happened, and now I know
He touched me, and made me whole"[30]*

The angel also spoke to Elijah one of the most powerful words of truth ever spoken to a human being: *"Get up and eat, for the journey is too much for you"* (19:7). I know you have felt the truth of these words in your own journey as I have felt them in mine more times than I can count. So often, I am guilty of running on empty and ignoring the check engine light on the inner dashboard of my soul. **Without regular rest, nourishment, and God's fresh touch, even the best and strongest of us cannot complete what God has called us to.** When we violate God's gift of rest time and time again, the night will overcome us. Taking time to rest will help us recover. It will also give the Lord the opportunity to supernaturally provide for us while we simply trust Him.

The great news is that Elijah does recover and continues his mission. He receives God's direction and guidance for the rest of the journey. When we are frustrated and tempted to get on with things, we need to slow down. If we do, we usually discover that God has more He would like to say to us. He has more of Himself He wants us to experience.

Mike Mason, in his inspiring book, *Practicing the Presence of People,* tells of his friend Mike who went through a long period of unemployment. During this time, he was plagued with insecurity, doubts, and questions. What was he to do with all the time on his hands? Without working, how was he to justify his existence? One Sunday, his pastor happened to ask in the sermon, *"When you're praying, do you ever pause and ask God to speak to you?"*

A few days later, Mike was in his garden praying. Once

---

[30] United Methodist Hymnal (Nashville: Abingdon Press, 1989), 367.

again, his thoughts were taken up with the difficulties of unemployment. But recalling his pastor's comment, Mike paused and asked God to speak to him. Immediately the Lord said, *"This is a time to focus on your wife and children. Learn to love them more deeply. Work is of very little importance to me. What's important to me is people."* [31]

This thought washed over Mike with a wave of freshness and relief. God had given him a job! Instead of feeling anxious about not having work, now Mike was free to focus on the most important work of all. He had just been given permission to love.

It seems that our pace keeps us from receiving love and from truly giving love to others. **To slow is to hear God's call to love again deeply.** Love gives both present significance and eternal meaning to work, and more importantly, to life. Brother Lawrence, a sixteenth-century monk once wrote, *"Count as lost each day you have not used loving God."*[32]

We need to ask why we resist slowing down or becoming still. Nancie Carmichael shares her answer to this question. *"On a long walk by the lake the Lord seemed to say, 'Be like a lake – still! Why did I resist the stillness so? I think it was because that is where I had to listen to the pain that I was so creative at avoiding and look at my less-than-perfect life, look at my disappointments and grieve my losses. I was afraid of the stillness because I didn't want to admit that my attempts at perfection were to mask the pain inside – which is exactly where God wanted to pour His love and grace.'"* [33]

---

[31] Mike Mason. *Practicing the Presence of People: How We Learn to Love* (Colorado Springs: Waterbrook Press, 1999), 40-41.
[32] Brother Lawrence and Harold J. Chadwick. *The Practice of the Presence of God* (Gainesville: Bridge-Logos Publishers, 2000), 34.
[33] John Maxwell, Tommy Barnett, Jill Briscoe, and Nancie Carmichael. *The Desert Experience: Personal Reflections on Finding God's Presence and Promise in Hard Times* (Nashville: Thomas Nelson Publishers, 2001), 71-72.

It sounds possible that choosing not to slow down is a way to push back the pain without facing it, a way to avoid dealing with how unmanageable our lives have become.

"...it is hard to stop in the middle of the muddle in order to listen to Him. But if you don't stop in the middle of the muddle, you will soon find you have a muddle in your middle – your stomach will be all tied up in knots." [34]

The storm was so bad that frightful night that I was forced to slow down. I couldn't go faster if I wanted to. But the beauty was that I was progressing towards home by going slower. Listen to some of the benefits I discovered on that frightful night:

- The night reminded me of how much things were beyond my control and how I needed help and rescue. I realized that my most used approach in life had been to grasp problems rather than surrender problems. I asked God to move me from clenched fists to open hands, from control to relinquishment, to unhook me from my anxious efforts to control outcomes. He wants us to trust Him and rest in allowing His plan to unfold.

- The night forced me to pay attention. It was said that the early church fathers used to say, *"The thing God wants from us most is our attention."* May He be the focal point of our thoughts and affections.

- The night stripped me of distractions. We live in not only a world of mass destruction but also mass distraction. *"Our culture is about distraction – numbing oneself. There is no self-reflection, no sitting still. It's absolutely exhausting. People don't want their lives fixed. Nobody wants their problems solved. Their dramas. Their distractions. Their stories*

---

[34] John Maxwell, Tommy Barnett, Jill Briscoe, and Nancie Carmichael. *The Desert Experience: Personal Reflections on Finding God's Presence and Promise in Hard Times* (Nashville: Thomas Nelson Publishers, 2001), 41.

resolved. Their messes cleaned up. Because what would they have left? Just the big, scary unknown." [35]

- The night forced me to be honest about what's inside myself, my feelings, emotions, loves, and fears. Driving down that slippery interstate, I found myself instantly in touch with the people and things that really mattered to me. And my trivial pursuits and old perspectives were dying by the dozen.

- The night helps us hear God. Sometimes God's voice of sanity can break in and be heard through the cacophony of violent and disturbing voices.

The poet W.H. Auden wrote, *"It is where we are wounded that God speaks to us."* [36] God speaks to us through our pain.

C.S. Lewis writes, *"Pain is the megaphone of God. God whispers to us in our pleasures, speaks in our conscience, but shouts in our pains – it is His megaphone to rouse a deaf world"* [37] We need to see pain as a gift – it tells us that something is up inside of us that needs some help or healing.

I think God may give us winter to help slow us down. The only time our family speeds up in winter is when Buddy, our miniature Border Collie, goes on his walks. His greatest passion is his long walks which are shortened in the cold of winter. He doesn't care what the weather is, but we do. I want to let you in on a secret. Buddy doesn't really like to walk that much; what he really likes is to sniff! A dog's sense of smell is thousands of times more sensitive than ours. It's how they interpret their world. When our boys

---

[35] David Greenfield. Retrieved from http://www.quotehd.com.
[36] John Maxwell, Tommy Barnett, Jill Briscoe, and Nancie Carmichael. *The Desert Experience: Personal Reflections on Finding God's Presence and Promise in Hard Times* (Nashville: Thomas Nelson Publishers, 2001), 72.
[37] C.S. Lewis. *The Problem of Pain* (New York: Harper Collins, 1940), 91.

walk him in winter, they are in a hurry to get done with the walk; because they don't understand what Tonya, my wife, understands – that Buddy has an urgent longing to sniff. She slows down and lets him sniff every mailbox, telephone pole, and neighbor's yard. He is delighted when he gets his long walk in! His tail wags instinctively and incessantly, praising God.

I hope you are taking time to sniff, to slow down, to stop and smell the roses especially if you are navigating a night in your life. **Don't be in such a hurry to get through it that you miss out on the gifts God has for you while you are in it!** If you slow down, you will be blessed with God's gift of marvelous margin where healing and restoration can happen. You just may pick up the scent, the fragrance of God's presence along the way that will sustain you through a tough day or a terrible season. You just may hear God's voice again!

Jesus stands at the door of our hearts inviting us to slow down and experience Him more and more. We can do this as we discover that our value and worth is in Christ alone.

"God is speaking in the night. The darkness is not a tragedy. The tragedy would be for us not to hear what God was saying to us there." [38]

---

[38] John Maxwell, Tommy Barnett, Jill Briscoe, and Nancie Carmichael. *The Desert Experience: Personal Reflections on Finding God's Presence and Promise in Hard Times* (Nashville: Thomas Nelson Publishers, 2001), 72.

Questions for Thought And Discussion

Chapter 3 – Creeping Along

1. When you are anxious or weary, are you more likely to speed up or slow down the pace of your life?

2. Does it frustrate you to go slower than you want to?

3. Have you ever been at a place and time in your life when you knew you were at your breaking point? Reflect on this. How did it feel, and what did you do about it?

4. Have you recently gone through or are you now going through a job or employment transition? What does this feel like to you?

Nancie Carmichael suggests that she resists slowing down because it would require her to listen to her pain and grieve her losses.

5. Why do you think you resist slowing down?

I write, *"We need to see pain as a gift – it tells us that something is up inside of us that needs some help or healing."*

6. Take a moment to thank God for your pain. Share your pain with Him in detail and ask Him to use it for His purposes in your life.

7. Where is it that you need God to pour out His love and grace on your life the most?

Chapter 4
Unfamiliar Roads

Please continue navigating the night with me as I putter and slide along in my little Volkswagen through a winter storm traveling from Music City [Nashville, TN] to the Holy City [Wilmore, KY].

I wrote in my journal: *"Every road I recognized and had traveled many times before was closed, and I was rerouted onto unfamiliar roads. I had no clue where I was..."*

We all seem to have a love for the familiar: Mom's dressing is what we like; we are more comfortable in our bed; there is nothing like our old house shoes broken in and conformed perfectly to our feet; our hometown newspaper, our favorite restaurant or spot in church.

We like familiar roads. There is a comfort level of driving on roads we know. We put it on automatic pilot and go. There is uncomfortable anxiety driving on roads we don't know.

I will never forget our experience when Tonya and I first married. We were taking a long road trip to a distant state to visit some friends who had just moved. We hadn't been married long, and I was still trying to impress her. I was obsessed with everything going perfectly. Since we had no GPS system then, I purchased a new road Atlas, highlighted my proposed course, confirmed the directions with my friend, wrote everything down, prayed for traveling mercies before leaving, and set out with complete confidence. We were cruising along making great progress until we got to a huge barricade with no warning whatsoever that read: **"Road Closed for Repair."** There were no detour signs, and I couldn't figure out an alternate route because the county roads weren't listed on my new map.

The only thing that went perfectly from that point on was my perfect exposure of idiocy and impatience. Tonya saw a side of me that she had never seen. Not knowing where I was going caused me to panic, and I transferred my anxiety onto her. **I am learning that pain that is not transformed will be transmitted to others.**[39] Flustered, I said with an attitude to my new bride, *"How about helping me? I can't drive and figure out a way for us to get there too."* Being lost was more than I could take, and I was unraveling. I was hot. I could see in her face her mind asking the question, *"What have I gotten myself into marrying this guy?"* I was forced to slow down, calm down, and ask Tonya to forgive me. I am thankful that she was generous to do so! I ended up stopping four times to ask people for directions. I even made some new friends by having to stop and ask for help. Finally, we arrived at our friend's beautiful place and had a wonderful week.

Difficult roads often lead to beautiful destinations!

The joy of familiarity was partly the inspiration for the writing of the song made so popular by John Denver, *"Take Me Home Country Roads."* Not only is the song the anthem for an entire state, but it resonates with our love for familiar things.

I've heard it said that *"The familiar is by far the most beautiful."* I don't know about this, but it's at least the most comfortable and cherished.

Sometimes, God calls us out of the familiar into the unfamiliar. There are seasons and times when we are placed in the valley of uncertainty when our faith is stretched beyond our comfort zones.

In Genesis 12, God calls Abram *"to leave his country, his people, and his father's household and go to the land I will*

---

[39] Sharon Cash. Presentation at Christ Church Memphis, Memphis, Tennessee, October 17, 2022.

show you" (Genesis 12:1).

In Joshua 3, God called the Israelites to cross the Jordan River into the unfamiliar territory before they could enter the Promised Land. Their comfort zones were being stretched. God gives them specific instructions to follow "*since you have never been this way before*" (3:4).

In Matthew 4:18-22, Jesus called four fishermen to follow him, and they didn't really know what that meant. Jesus calls Peter and Andrew doing what they were familiar with – "*they were casting a net into the lake…*" when Jesus says, "*Come, follow me and I will make you fishers of men*" (4:19). **They were fixing to travel some roads they'd never been on before.**

"*At once, they left their nets and followed Him*" (4:20).

Then Jesus called two brothers, James and John, sons of Zebedee (a man of resources). They were in a boat with their father, Zebedee, repairing their nets. Jesus called them, "*and immediately they left the boat and their father and followed Him*" (Matthew 4:18-22).

They left their nets, left their boat, left their father, and everything they had known. They left their fishing business to help others find God.

Leaving the familiar is part of the nature of Christian discipleship. Dietrich Bonhoeffer, a martyr executed by the Nazis in 1945, reminds us that "*the old life is left behind, and completely surrendered,*" and "*the disciple is dragged out of his relative security into a life of absolute insecurity.*" [40]

"The cross is laid on every Christian, the leaving of all and going with the incarnate Son of God." [41]

---

[40] Dietrich Bonhoeffer. *The Cost of Discipleship* (New York: Collier, 1937), 62.
[41] Dietrich Bonhoeffer. *The Cost of Discipleship* (New York: Collier, 1937), 99.

All believers face times of uncertainty when risk and sacrifice are mandatory. I don't know what unfamiliar road you might find yourself on. The Lord might take you out of the country and put you in the city or take you out of the city and put you in the country. You might have to face the road of the death of a loved one. You might hit the bumps of divorce you never wanted or asked for. Maybe your child will be diagnosed with autism. You might be in a long lull between jobs. Your faith might be stretched when someone hurts you with their words and actions, and you are called to forgive and push past the grudge and bitterness to freedom not based on how others treat you but how much God has forgiven you. **There are many long winter roads of all kinds.**

I do know this – every child of God will be called to trust Him to guide them through life situations they have never encountered before.

Deeper faith is made possible through these situations. **God uses the seeming impasses of our lives as bridges to growth, but we must step out by faith.**

Bonhoeffer said, *"If we refuse to follow and stay behind, we will not learn how to believe."* [42] Our faith grows as we are willing to go with God into the unknown and unfamiliar.

Jesus said to Peter after he was recalled, *"You will go where you do not want to go"* (John 21:18). Jesus predicts a season in Peter's life that will call for total dependence on others and even death in old age. Peter will come to a time when he will not be in control but must depend on others.

Periods of uncertainty are often experienced in the Christian life, but the willingness to accept this reality as a gift may determine a disciple's growth.

---

[42] Dietrich Bonhoeffer. *The Cost of Discipleship* (New York: Collier, 1937), 67.

Henri Nouwen echoes this truth when he writes, *"To grow in the Spirit of the Lord means to be led to the same powerless place where Jesus was led: Calvary, the cross. It means the road of downward mobility in the midst of an upwardly mobile world."* [43]

As you travel this unfamiliar road, remember God is with you and as God told Joshua, I will show you the way – seek my presence and power, and *"then you will know which way to go, since you have never passed this way before"* (3:4).

When the brilliant ethicist, John Kavanaugh, went to work for three months at *"the house of the dying"* in Calcutta, he sought a clear answer as to how best to spend the rest of his life. On the first morning there, he met Mother Teresa. She asked him, *"What can I do for you?"*

Kavanaugh asked her to pray for him. *"What do you want me to pray for?"* she asked.

He voiced the request that he had been carrying for thousands of miles from the United States: *"Pray that I have clarity."*

She said firmly, *"No, I will not do that."*

When he asked her why, she said, *"Clarity is the last thing you are clinging to and must let go of."*

When Kavanaugh commented that she always seemed to have the clarity he longed for, she laughed and said, *"I have never had clarity; what I have always had is trust. So I will pray that you trust God."* [44]

Hannah Smith once wrote, *"We must understand that our*

---

[43] Stephen Seamands. *A Conversation with Jesus: Renewing Your Passion for Ministry* (Wheaton: Victor, 1994), 59.
[44] Brennan Manning. *Ruthless Trust: The Ragamuffin's Path to God* (New York: Harper Collins, 2000), 16.

God has all knowledge and all wisdom...and all love towards us...He may guide us into paths where He knows great blessings are awaiting us, but which to the shortsighted human eyes around us seem sure to result in confusion and loss." [45]

In Isaiah 42, God calls Israel both blind and deaf. He says you have seen many things but have paid no attention. Despite this, He says I will work majestic and miraculous wonders for you and help you do what you cannot do for yourselves. Listen to **GOD'S 6 "I WILL" statements.**

"<u>I will lead</u> the blind by ways they have not known, along unfamiliar paths <u>I will guide</u> them; <u>I will turn</u> the darkness into light before them and (<u>I will</u> understood) make the rough places smooth. These are things <u>I will do</u>; <u>I will not</u> forsake them" (42:16).

Notice how active God is in the nights of our lives.

"I don't think God puts us on this earth so we can be afraid of stepping into the unknown. Isn't tomorrow an unknown even if we all stay right here where tradition is kept, and every piece of ground is familiar?" [46]

For almost forty years, I joyfully remember turning off the rural Alabama highway onto a sandy road leading up to Pawpaw's house on the hill. I knew there would eventually come a day when Pawpaw wouldn't be there; I just didn't think it would be that day. Unfortunately, we almost always think in terms of tomorrow. But on that day, February 12, 2010, the Lord received my beloved grandfather into His eternal presence.

The landscape of forty acres was clothed in an all-white garment of snow, and Pawpaw's Pond was almost frozen

---

[45] Bob Benson and Michael Benson. *The Christian's Secret of a Happy Life: Disciplines for the Inner Life* (Nashville: Thomas Nelson, 1989), 226.
[46] Cindy Woodsmall. *For Every Season* (Colorado Springs: WaterBrook, 2013).

solid. As my brother, Chad, and I drove up this long winter road, it came to me that although I had traveled this road many times, death made it seem very different today. Death is a transition for the dead and the living, for those who go and those who stay.

I rejoice for my grandfather, who is now breathing heaven's air after struggling to get a good breath for the past few years. As my family and I face this transition, I take comfort in the words of Joshua to the Israelites before they crossed the flood waters of the chilly Jordan: *"follow the ark of the covenant (which means God's Presence) in order that you may know the way you should go, for you have not passed this way before"* (Joshua 3:4).

God's Presence helps us cross every road of uncertainty. God never calls us to something He doesn't promise to lead us through. As you come to new roads you have never traveled before, seek His Presence. In all the uncertainty, He will help you know how you should go. Crossover looking for springtime. It's just ahead of every long winter road!

Prayer:

*"My Lord God, I have no idea where I am going.
I do not see the road ahead of me.
I cannot know for certain where it will end.
Nor do I really know myself, and the fact that I think I am following your will does not mean that I am actually doing so.
But I believe that the desire to please you does in fact please you.
And I hope I have that desire in all that I am doing.
I hope that I will never do anything apart from that desire.
And I know that if I do this you will lead me by the right road,
though I know nothing about it.
Therefore, I will trust you always though I may seem to be lost and in the shadow of death. I will not fear, for you are*

ever with me, and you will never leave me to face my perils alone." [47]

---

[47] Thomas Merton. *Thoughts in Solitude* (New York: Farrar, Straus and Giroux Publishers, 1999), 79.

Questions for Thought And Discussion

Chapter 4 – Unfamiliar Roads

1. Are you familiar with John Denver's song, *"Take Me Home Country Roads?"* What emotions do you experience when you think of "home?"

2. Would you say you are more likely to actively resist change or openly welcome it? Why?

3. Bonhoeffer says that Christian discipleship calls us *"to leave the old life behind..."* In what ways have you had to leave your old life behind? Are there ways the old life is still hanging on?

4. What do you think of Mother Teresa's response to John Kavanaugh when he asked her to pray for clarity in his next steps? She said to him, *"I will not do that...but I will pray that you trust God."* Do you see her point?

5. Would you agree that change or being called to face something unfamiliar is essential to learning how to trust God?

6. Spend some time with Thomas Merton's prayer at the end of the chapter. Ask God to put in you the spirit of honesty and trust that Merton shows in his prayer.

Chapter 5
Navigational Means of Grace

Before I share the conclusion of my story in the next chapter, I want to share some of the ways the Lord has helped me navigate the night.

Being plunged into darkness on that bone-chilling night, I became increasingly aware of my sense of fear and lostness. I realized how desperately I needed God's comfort for my fear and guidance for my lostness.

It is common to fear the dark, and I sure did that night.

I feared the darkness of the winter storm I was driving through and the darkness of disorientation during many of the ordinary days of my life.

I'm like the little boy playing one afternoon outdoors. He used his mother's broom as a horse and had a wonderful time until it began to get dark.

He left the broom on the back porch. His mother was cleaning up the kitchen after supper when she realized her broom was missing. She asked the little boy about the broom, and he told her where it was.

She then asked him to please go get it. The little boy informed his mom that he feared the dark and didn't want to go out to get the broom.

His mother smiled and said, *"The Lord is out there too, son, don't be afraid."* The little boy opened the back door just a little and said, *"Lord, if you are out there, please hand me the broom."*

Sometimes I've had to go to God like a child and simply tell Him that I was afraid and needed His help. **I'm learning**

that God is present in the places where my fears live! Perhaps, you are afraid of something right now. Don't try and fight your fears without God's help. **He is present where your fears live too!**

I'm finding great freedom in going to God with my fears, not hiding them but confiding in Him by naming them. Almost every time I take this courageous step, I experience a holy exchange – God takes my fears and replaces them with His love. *"His perfect love drives out (unhealthy – my emphasis) fear"* (1 John 4:18).

Despite my fear, I remember feeling an abounding sense of gratitude for my little car that night. It seemed a very close friend, a refuge, and a shelter from the storm. It kept me warm and dry. Its protection provided a real sense of God's presence and a helpful reminder that He had been my refuge throughout every day of my life, especially those that had felt like a long twilight. Somehow, He had sustained me and preserved me. From the depths of my soul sprang memories of many times when God showed up with gifts of reorientation and caused the sun to shine again in my life.

"God is our refuge and strength, an ever-present help in trouble. Therefore, we will not fear, though the earth give way, and the mountains fall into the heart of the sea…" - Psalm 46:1-2

In addition to my fear, I have a terrible sense of direction.

I'm kind of like the senior citizen who was driving down the freeway when his cell phone rang.

Answering, he heard his wife's voice urgently warning him, *"Herman, I just heard on the news that there's a car going the wrong way on the Interstate – Please be careful!"*

"Heck," said Herman, *"It's not just one car. It's hundreds of them!"*[48]

Life can come at us so fast and furiously that we don't even know what direction we're going in.

I'm learning that God is also present in the places where I am lost or in need of direction! Perhaps, you feel lost without direction. **Be encouraged.**

David asks, *"Where can I go from Your Spirit? Where can I flee from Your presence? If I go up to the heavens, you are there; If I make my bed in the depths, you are there…even the darkness will not be dark to you; the night will shine like the day, for darkness is as light to you"* (Psalm 139:7-8, 12).

In our fear, God comforts us by saying, *"So do not fear, for I am with you; do not be dismayed, for I am your God; I will strengthen you and help you; I will uphold you with my righteous right hand"* (Isaiah 41:10).

In our need for direction, God says, *"I will instruct you and teach you in the way you should go; I will counsel you and watch over you"* (Psalm 32:8). We must live into these promises.

Growing up, my family moved frequently because Dad was a traveling salesman and an entrepreneur. Although we had many transitions and changed houses often, one thing never changed. Dad's old 200-foot, heavy-duty, green hose always went with us. He still has it. It was the delivery system for fresh water to sprinkle the lawn, wash the cars, windows, and sidewalks, or take a refreshing drink on a hot summer day. I think of that hose as Old Faithful! Gallon after gallon of fresh water flowed through it.

---

[48] "The Wrong Way." Jokes of the Day. Accessed at http://www.jokesoftheday.net/joke-Wrong-Way/2014042140.

God's love comes to us in various ways that are sometimes called means of grace. Grace is the free gift of God's love constantly flowing through Jesus Christ. It never runs dry. It's always there. It's God's Old Faithful! It's the power of God working in us to give us a transformed life. It's the way God supernaturally delivers what our hearts need most. Through His fresh supply of grace, God sustains and strengthens our faith and hope and carries us through every night until we land safely home.

God has many ways to deliver the flow of His grace. Here are some ways or means by which His grace has flowed to me as I've navigated the night.

1. Remembering – Remembering the Lord, who He is, and what He has done is a powerful means of grace to overcome darkness. Remembering Him is more than an exercise of the mind. It also is a longing of the heart to encounter and reencounter the Living Lord. Remembering is about thinking of Him and longing for Him.

"My soul is downcast within me; therefore, I will remember you (with my mind and heart)"
- Psalm 42:6

"On my bed I remember you (with my mind and heart); I think of you through the watches of the night..." - Psalm 63:6

Both times, the text says, *"I remember you...,"* not what about me?

When navigating the night, it is my frequent tendency to become so self-absorbed in my difficulties and problems that I get locked up in the prison house of self.

I often pray for God to deliver me from self-preoccupation with my problems, my stuff, my life, my ministry, my, my, my...It is easy to become the center of our universe.

'If we look at the world for too long, we will be distressed; if we look at ourselves for too long, we will be depressed; but if we look at Jesus, we will be at rest.'[49]

Remembering the Lord, setting our attention and affection on Him, liberates us from the prison of self-preoccupation.

"To focus on how I'm doing more than what Christ has done is Christian narcissism."[50] Our self-focus shrivels, shrinks, and dies in the face of the power of the cross of Christ and His glorious resurrection. Whatever our struggle is, it doesn't define reality. Who God is and what He's done in Christ is always more real than what we are dealing with.

Remembering Him involves meditating on God's character. *"Because of the Lord's great love, we are not consumed, for His compassions never fail. They are new every morning, great is your faithfulness"* (Lamentations 3:22-23). Once we get a fresh revelation and vision of who God is, no giant that comes against us looks as enormous.

Remembering Him gets our minds off our inability and on His ability. Dr. E. Stanley Jones once wrote, *"The whole secret to abundant living can be summed up in this sentence: 'Not your responsibility but your response to His ability!'"* [51]

---

[49] Debbie McDaniel. "10 Powerful Quotes from Corrie Ten Boom." Crosswalk.com. Retrieved from https://www.crosswalk.com/faith/spiritual-life/inspiring-quotes/40-powerful-quotes-from-corrie-ten-boom.html.
[50] Tullian Tchividjian. *Jesus + Nothing = Everything* (Wheaton: Crossway Books, 2011).
[51] E. Stanley Jones. *Abundant Living: 364 Daily Devotionals* (Nashville: Abingdon, 1942), 183.

> *"How precious to me are your thoughts, O God!*
> *How vast is the sum of them!*
> *Were I to count them, they would outnumber the grains of sand.*
> *When I awake, I am still with you"* - Psalm 139:17-18

Since God's mind is so much on us, it only makes sense that our minds should be so much on Him.

2. Singing – Singing to the Lord, and praising Him, is a powerful means of grace to overcome darkness.
I remember, as a little boy, seeing a bird fly into our church gymnasium during a special service as my mother beautifully sang, *"His Eye Is on the Sparrow."* It flew in on a high soprano note of praise and made laps around the gym. It put on an aerial show! The large crowd marveled in joyful wonder at God's confirming sign. The presence of God was so palpable that morning that I believe all darkness had to flee.

> *"Because you are my help, I sing in the shadow of your wings."* - Psalm 63:7

> *"By day the Lord directs His love, at night His song is with me – a prayer to the God of my life."*
> - Psalm 42:8

I like things strong. Strong coffee, strong flavors and seasonings, strong lemonade not watered down. I like to pucker when I taste, but often I am aware of the weakness of my praise and the silence of my song. Sometimes, my song is not strong enough to fight against the many faces and voices of the night. In a lot of churches, the choir is dying out. In a lot of people, the choir is dying out. **We must get the choir within going again. Doctrine is important, but so is doxology!** Opening my mouth, especially when I don't feel like it, as an act of willing worship and praise for who God is and what He has done almost always opens my heart to receive whatever I need from Him.

Pastor Paul Lawler often says, *"There are two times when we should offer God praise: when we feel like and when we don't!"*

It's good to come into His presence with singing, with strong praise and worship (Psalm 100:2).

Brandon Lake's album, *House of Miracles*, includes a song entitled, "Gratitude" that has some powerful lyrics that call us to passionate praise:

"So come on, my soul
Oh, don't you get shy on me
Lift up your song
'Cause you've got a lion inside of those lungs
Get up and praise the Lord"[52]

A man in one of the churches I served complained regularly and irritatingly, *"I am here for the preaching. The singing is preliminary and doesn't matter."* He always came late, right before the preaching. I told him the singing and the preaching went together like peanut butter and jelly, but he was never convinced. He was too busy to sing and praise and lacked the desire to bless the Lord, yet his life was full of bad stress and was one big mess.

"I remembered my songs in the night" (Psalm 77:6). This beautiful verse links remembering and singing together as powerful weapons. There is power in praise.

I love verse 2 of *When Morning Gilds the Skies*:

---

[52] Brandon Lake. "Gratitude." Track 7 on *House of Miracles*. Bethel Music. 2020.

*"The night becomes as day when from the heart we say:
May Jesus Christ be praised!
The powers of darkness fear when this sweet chant they hear:
May Jesus Christ be praised!"*[53]

Strong praise disarms and dispels the darkness.

"In darkness as in the light, praise was the dominant note of Jesus' life, and not the cross itself could silence it."[54]

"I will praise the Lord who counsels me; even at night my heart instructs me." - Psalm 16:7

---

*"Let everything that has breath praise the Lord."
- Psalm 150:6*

"I will praise the Lord all my life; I will sing praise to my God as long as I live." - Psalm 146:2

"I will bless the Lord at all times; His praise will always be on my lips." - Psalm 34:1

Something transformational happens when we begin to sing <u>to God</u>, not just <u>about Him</u>. *"About midnight Paul and Silas were praying and singing hymns to God, and the other prisoners were listening to them. Suddenly there was such a violent earthquake that the foundations of the prison were shaken. All at once, the prison doors flew open, and everybody's chains came loose"* (Acts 16:25-26). His power is released in us when we praise Him.

---

[53] *United Methodist Hymnal* (Nashville: Abingdon Press, 1989), 185.
[54] John W. Doberstein. *The Minister's Prayer Book* (London: Fortress Press, 1986).

The jailer and his whole household ended up getting saved because two of God's people in prison started singing. There are certainly times when life seems so heavy and dark that all we can do is sigh. But we must not forget to sing again: *"May Jesus Christ be praised!"*

3. Reading – Reading God's Word and letting God's Word read us are powerful means of grace to overcome darkness.

The Bible is the only book I know that reads me while I read it. *"It judges the thoughts and attitudes of (my) heart"* (Hebrews 4:12d). It reads my mind, motives, moods, and manners.

"Your Word is a lamp unto my feet and a light for my path." - Psalm 119:105

A few years ago, we were going on a long trip to Texas driving through the night when some dear friends, Jack and Sheila Beavers, who were scouts of the century being always prepared for anything, gave us a rescue kit that included an extra-large flashlight in case we broke down. Sheila said we always need to carry a light in the night. It doesn't take a lot of light to extinguish the night. When it comes to God's Word, we must come to it longing to meet Jesus in its pages, its promises, its principles, its precepts, but most of all in His person. All the Word points us to a living, loving person who longs to have a relationship with us. The light of His Word shines on us, in us, and through us.

The Bible is alive, it speaks to me; it has feet, it runs after me; it has hands, it lays hold of me – it guides me and turns me in the right direction.

"If we would dance our way into some deeper communion

with God, we must stop working on the Word, wherever it is found, and let the Word begin to work on us"[55]

The Psalmist writes, *"I have suffered much; preserve my life, O Lord, according to Your Word"* (119:107).

In the darkness of the night, I am learning that I can't fight the battle of the mind or emotions apart from the Word of God. The enemy wants us to just sit with our thoughts or the thoughts he has planted in us without shining the extra-large flashlight of God's Word, which the darkness cannot overcome (John 1:5).

"Never doubt in the dark what God told you in the light."[56]

4. Crying Out – Crying out to the Lord, pouring out our hearts in prayer, is a powerful means of grace to overcome darkness.

"Trust in Him at all times, O people; pour out your hearts to Him, for God is our refuge." - Psalm 62:8

"Arise, cry out in the night, as the watches of the night begin; pour out your heart like water in the presence of the Lord." - Lamentations 2:19

Notice the phrases *"cry out"* and *"pour out"* appear together in this verse. I'm not sure we can teach prayer. It seems it must be born out of a whole environment of felt need. In some ways, we must be driven to pray. **I am discovering that it is the nights of my life that provide the best classroom for learning how to cry out to God in prayer.**

---

[55] Robert Benson. *Living Prayer* (New York: TarcherPerigee Publishers, 1999).
[56] "V. Raymond Edman Quotes." *Good Reads.* Accessed from http://www.goodreads.com.

We must learn again to cry out to the true Source of our help.

Crying out to God suggests an intensity of spirit that affirms our dependence on God.

"I cry out with my whole heart...I cry out to You...save me...I cry for help." - Psalm 119:145-147

Years ago, on a visit to Cades Cove in the Smoky Mountains, I saw a mother bear and her cubs feasting in a row of wild cherry trees. Each climbed their own tree to pick it clean. It was so fun to watch! I was one of the first spectators, but soon a huge crowd gathered, making the cubs exceedingly nervous. As the crowd pressed in, they started fidgeting and crying out like babies. As soon as their cries reached Momma's ears, she came bolting down the cherry tree she was in to come to their aid. The crowd split in a thousand directions. People that hadn't run in years took off! Those cubs knew the source of their help, and their intense cry got momma's attention and everybody else's.

Crying out is not always an audible noise. It can also be an inward cry boiling over – a yearning and a burning after more of God, a deep desire for God to show up and do great and mighty things. Hannah cried out to God in prayer to make her barren womb fruitful without ever being heard by anyone but God (1 Samuel 1:12-16).

I heard an elderly African American lady once say, *"The trouble with lots of prayers is that they ain't got no suction."* She's not talking about tone or volume, but urgency and intensity! We need to drive our prayers into our doubts, fears, hurts, and every other problem we have.

Crying out to God distinguishes the faithful from the

unfaithful. Unfaithful Israel thought they knew God, but God said, *"You do not know Me because you do not cry out to Me from the heart"* (Hosea 7:14).

A composition teacher asked the class to write about an unusual event from the past week. One boy got up and read his essay. It began: *"Daddy fell in the well last week..."*

"My goodness!" the teacher said. *"Is he alright?"*

"He must be," said the boy. *"He stopped yelling for help yesterday."*

Some of us have quit crying out because we are discouraged and tired! *"The enemy uses the routine of adversity, the gradual decay of our hopes and loves, the quiet despair of ever overcoming the chronic temptations, with which we have again and again been defeated, to wear our souls out by attrition."*[57] **We lose heart!**

Pouring out prayer is the way we continue to keep our hearts alive in Him when things are hard. We tell God what is in us, not what ought to be in us! We pour every detail of our lives out to God. When we do this, we exchange our panic for His peace (Philippians 4:6-7). As we pour our heart out to Him, He pours His heart into us!

"It is sadly common for Jesus to become Someone we talk about rather than Someone we talk to."[58] We need to talk to Him and listen to Him. Have you ever paused in prayer and said, *"Lord, speak to me! I am listening!"*

Crying out prayer signals a deeper reliance on the ministry of the Holy Spirit, who *"helps us in our weakness"* by *"interceding for us with groans that words cannot express"* (Romans 8:26). As we navigate the night, we must invite

---

[57] C.S. Lewis. *The Screwtape Letters* (New York: Harper One, 2015).
[58] Chris Tiegreen and Walk Through Ministries. *The One Year At His Feet Devotional* (Carol Stream: Tyndale House Publishers, 2003), 280.

and trust the Holy Spirit to help us. That's who the Holy Spirit is – our Helper (John 14:26 NASB).[59] Jude encourages believers, *"But you, dear friends, build yourselves up in your most holy faith and pray in the Holy Spirit"* (1:20).

"Only where the Spirit is sighed for, cried for, and prayed for will He be present and newly active."[60]

5. Sowing – Sowing, scattering seed, is a powerful means of grace to overcome darkness.

"Those who sow in tears will reap with songs of joy."
- Psalm 126:5

"He who goes out weeping, carrying seed to sow, will return with songs of joy, carrying sheaves with him."
- Psalm 126:6

For many years I have made pilgrimages to different monasteries to cultivate silence. In the quietness, God seems to speak – or at least I am more able to hear. On a visit to Sacred Heart Convent in Cullman, Alabama, during a difficult stretch of OCD, my heart was inspired.

I walked right by her – that little nun planting flowers in the rain.

Sister Kathleen, every day of 80 dressed in her plastic rain cap, knelt along the sidewalk planting colorful Johnny-jump-ups. Drops of rain were still falling, and as I passed by, I said, *"That's commitment. I will recommend a raise!"*

---

[59] HOLY BIBLE: NEW AMERICAN STANDARD BIBLE (LaHabra: The Lockman Foundation, 1995).
[60] Karl Barth. *Evangelical Theology: An Introduction* (New York: Holt, Rinehart, and Winston, 1963), 58.

She laughed the most beautiful of laughs and kept right on planting.

The scene sent my heart soaring. How easy it is to quit sowing while it rains? We usually resolve to sow again someday when things get better – when the rain passes.

What a sacrifice to sow love when all we want is for someone to love us. It is hard to sow seed when we are the ones in need. Yet it is God's way. To sow is to help ourselves out of trouble and trial. I love the intentionality of the farmer spoken of in this Psalm: *"He who goes out weeping, carrying seed to sow..."* (Psalm 126:6). He doesn't let his weeping stop him.

Whatever you may be going through, remember to keep sowing love, acts of kindness, encouragement, faith, hope, and even tears. A joyful harvest is soon to come.

"Weeping may remain for a night; but rejoicing comes in the morning." - Psalm 30:5

"If you spend yourselves on behalf of the hungry and satisfy the needs of the oppressed, then your light will rise in the darkness, and your night will become like the noonday." - Isaiah 58:10

Dr. Karl Menninger was asked what a person should do if he felt a nervous breakdown beginning. He said, *"Lock up your house, go across the railroad tracks, and find someone in need, and do something for him."*[61]

6. Practicing – Practicing God's presence and the presence of people are powerful means of grace to overcome darkness.

---

[61] "Karl Menninger Quotes". Accessed from http://www.quotefancy.com.

"Be still before the Lord and wait patiently for Him."
- Psalm 37:7a

"Repent, then, and turn to God...that times of refreshing may come from the presence of the Lord."
- Acts 3:19

We need the presence of God during the night times. Mental and emotional darkness, and oppression of all kinds, are lifted by the presence of Christ.

I mentioned earlier that we live in a world of mass distraction. We allow too many things to interrupt our awareness of Jesus and our walk with Him.

A few winters ago, a ferocious storm made for an icy landscape. My three young sons and I gave up on making snowmen and built an ice fort! There was such a pond of ice beneath my feet that my weight could not break it...until the sun came out. Although temperatures were still below freezing, after just a few hours of sunshine, I could see and hear ice softening into slush and gigantic icebergs sliding off rooftops.

While taking shuffle steps across the top of our driveway, I heard a snap, crackle, pop noise that ran to the street. The ice ripped down the middle. The sun demonstrated its melting power to work beneath the surface to bring change.

Sometimes our lives feel like an icy landscape. We are imprisoned within our self-made ice forts or become victims to the dark nights of the soul.

But Zechariah prophesied of the Messiah that he called *"the SUNRISE from on high who shall visit us from heaven to shine on those living in darkness and in the shadow of death"* (Luke 1:78-79).

Jesus is the ice breaker! The presence and power of the Son bring heat and light to transform the unbreakable. His presence is such an indescribable gift because it changes us!

God's presence transforms our hearts. We need to get in it – pray for it, seek it, make time for it, value it, thank Him for it, love it, and linger in it until the icy landscapes of our hearts become like a warm, flowery meadow teeming with life. Do you ever schedule an early morning or a date night with the Lord? It's amazing that the Person we need to be with the most is the One we sometimes neglect or avoid the most. We really don't know how to be with others until we are first with Him.

We need the presence of people during the nights of our lives. And thankfully, God allows us to be a helpful presence to fellow strugglers during their dark nights.

All of us need a few friends who truly know us and are not impressed by us but love us for who we are and are willing to help us journey through our nights.

An unknown author tells the story of two horses who stood in a field just up the road from his house. From a distance, each horse looked like any other horse. But if you stopped your car or walked by, you would notice something amazing. Looking into the eyes of one horse would disclose that he was blind. His owner chose not to have him put down but made a good home for him. This alone is amazing.

If you stand nearby and listen, you will hear a bell. Looking around for the source of the sound, you will see that it comes from the smaller horse in the field.

Attached to the horse's halter is a small bell. It lets the blind friend know where the horse is, so he can follow.

As you stand and watch these two friends, you'll see that the horse with the bell is always checking on the blind horse and that the blind horse will listen for the bell and then slowly walk to where the other horse is, trusting that he will not be led astray.

When the horse with the bell returns to the shelter of the barn each evening, it stops occasionally and looks back, making sure that the blind friend isn't too far behind to hear the bell.

Like the owners of these two horses, God does not throw us away just because we are not perfect or walking through some tough times or dark nights, but He watches over us and even brings others into our lives to help us when we are in need.

Sometimes, we are the blind horse guided by the ringing bell from those whom God places in our lives.
Other times we are the guide horse, helping others to find their way.

Please, listen for my bell, and I'll listen for yours!

"Love cures people – both the ones who give it and the ones who receive it."[62]

"In every encounter, we either give life or we drain it. There is NO neutral exchange."[63]

7 Thanking – Thanking the Lord at all times and having a gratitude attitude are powerful means of grace to overcome darkness.

---

[62] "Karl Menninger Quotes." Accessed from http://www.brainyquote.com.
[63] "Brennan Manning Quotes." Accessed from http://www.quotefancy.com.

> *"...give thanks in all circumstances, for this is God's will for you in Christ Jesus." - 1 Thessalonians 5:18*

Two friends bumped into one another in town – one of them looked downhearted, almost on the verge of tears. His friend asked, *"What has the world done to you, my old friend?"* He said, *"Let me tell you. Three weeks ago, an uncle died and left me $40,000 dollars."* His friend said, *"That's a lot of money."*

"But two weeks ago, a cousin I never even knew died, leaving me $85,000 dollars free and clear." His friend said, *"Sounds like you've been blessed."*

"You don't understand!" He interrupted. *"Last week, my great aunt passed away. I inherited almost a quarter of a million dollars."* Now his friend was confused and said, *"Then why do you look so gloomy?"*

He said, "THIS WEEK – NOTHING!"

It's so easy to become forgetful and unthankful recipients of God's good gifts! Elizabeth Elliott once said, *"It is always possible to be thankful for what is given rather than to complain about what is not given – one or the other becomes a habit of life."*[64]

The Jewish Germans refer to the habit of a complaining soul, an ungrateful spirit as KAVETCHING. It's a kind of personal griping session: *"Oh, why did this have to happen to me of all people? It's always something! Everything always goes wrong...When it rains, it pours...I'm doing all I can to live right but nothing good comes my way..."*

"Hell begins with a grumbling mood, always complaining,

---

[64] "Elizabeth Elliott Quotes." Accessed from http://www.quotefancy.com.

always blaming...in each of us there is something growing, which will BE hell unless it is nipped in the bud."[65]

We've got to nip a griping heart of ingratitude in the bud.

God has two dwellings: one is in heaven, and the other is in a thankful heart!

Paul says, *"give thanks in all circumstances..."* "All" means that **gratitude or thanksgiving is meant to be inclusive and attentive.**

The late Henri Nouwen wrote: *"To be grateful for the good things that happen in our lives is easy, but to be grateful for all our lives – the good as well as the bad, the moments of joy as well as the moments of sorrow, the successes as well as the failures...that requires some hard spiritual work. Still, we are only grateful people when we can say thank you to all that has brought us to the present moment."*[66]

It's easy not to include all our lives in our thanksgiving list. It's also easy to be so busy and preoccupied with life that we become inattentive to the gifts that arrive each day. We simply stop paying attention.

"To be made aware and alert to the presence of God manifested in a piece of music heard on the car radio, a daffodil, a kiss, an encouraging word from a friend, a thunderstorm, a newborn baby, a sunrise or a sunset, a falling leaf, a rainbow, or the magnificent lines on the face of an aging relative requires an inner freedom from self...."[67]

The marvels of God are everywhere. Without a grateful heart, a gratitude attitude, we will fail to see most things

---

[65] C.S. Lewis. *The Great Divorce* (New York: MacMillan Publishing, 1978), 77-78.
[66] Brennan Manning. *Ruthless Trust: The Ragamuffin's Path to God* (New York: Harper Collins, 2000), 31.
[67] Brennan Manning. *Ruthless Trust: The Ragamuffin's Path to God* (New York: Harper Collins, 2000), 32.

but our problems.

This list of seven is not exhaustive but provides examples of God's gifts of grace that help us navigate the night. May His fresh supply of living water flow through you as you remember, sing, read, pray, sow, practice the presence, and give thanks. May the grace of God multiply in your life and make you whole as His light overcomes the darkness.

"Stir up the gifts of grace within you, and God will give you even more grace."[68]

---

[68] This quote has been attributed to John Wesley.

Questions for Thought And Discussion

Chapter 5 – Navigational Means of Grace

1. Did you fear the dark when you were a child? Can you remember any specific experiences?

2. Do you believe God is present to help you where your fears live? Are you in the habit of sharing them with Him?

3. Do you feel that life has come at you fast and furiously or just about right? Explain or reflect on your answer.

4. Do you trust God to be present with you in the places where you need direction and guidance?

5. Meditate on Psalm 32:8, *"I will instruct you in the way you should go; I will counsel you and watch over you."*

God's grace involves His power working in our lives to transform us. I compare God's grace to a faithful old hose that delivers living water to dry places to satisfy them or to dirty places to clean them.

6. How do you describe God's grace? What might you compare it to?

7. Out of the seven ways I mention (remember, sing, read, pray, sow, practice the presence, and give thanks) that God's grace flows to us, which one(s) do you find it easiest to practice? Which one(s) are hardest for you to practice?

8. Do you enjoy practicing the presence of God and the presence of people?

Stay on Board
Chapter 6

A hillbilly in East Tennessee left his mountain home and moved to the big city of Chicago and finally to New York City. After landing a seat on the stock exchange, he never returned to his mountain home. One day, he received a call from his family saying, *"Papa is dying – can you come home?"*

He apologized and said, *"I am so sorry; I can't leave. I am about to close a big deal. Give Papa a great funeral. Don't be cheap about it. Send me the bill for the expenses, and I'll pay for it."*

About a week later, he heard from his family, *"Papa died. We gave him the greatest funeral this mountain community ever saw. Here's the bill, $10,017.38."* The out-of-town son cut a check for $10,017.38. The next month, he received a bill for $17.38. He paid this bill, but another for $17.38 came in the mail the following month. For the next six months, he received a bill for $17.38. After this, he called one of his brothers and asked, *"Why do I keep getting a monthly bill for $17.38 listed as funeral expenses?"*

His brother replied, *"Well, you said to bury Papa, and don't be cheap about it. We spent $10,000 on the funeral. The $17.38 a month is for the rented tuxedo we buried him in."*[69]

Not every experience has a conclusion.

Thankfully, mine does, and a positive one at that.

At nearly 2:30 a.m., almost nine grueling hours after leaving Nashville, I pulled my faithful and valiant

---

[69] Hank H. Russell. *How to Live Life Laughing!* (Gainesville: Maranatha Publications, 2010), 162.

Volkswagen into my apartment driveway in Wilmore, Kentucky. The trip took almost three times as long as the normal three and a half hours. The snow and ice were still falling, and the temperature was frigid. My eyes were bloodshot, shoulders tight, neck sore, back stiff, and arms limp like a cowboy who had just finished riding a bull for eight seconds. It also dawned on me that I had never gone to the bathroom this entire time. That was a miracle for me as I joke about having a 20-mile-bladder. I can hardly go further than 20 miles without stopping for a bathroom break. The thought of stopping never crossed my mind.

Although every part of me was completely exhausted and my energy was depleted, my heart was thankful. God had led me through the night to home. I felt I must have had an angel escort. It was so surreal, but before I got out of the car and my feet hit the ice and snow, I thanked the Lord for His help and for my life, family, home, ministry, and anything else I could think of. And I committed to a more devoted life. I even vowed not to complain or grumble ever again. Regretfully, I have not always kept this promise, but I continue to renew my resolve.

When I walked into my apartment, I sat and sobbed, a mixture of tears of relief and gratitude. That night, I stayed up the entire night. It was the only night in my life I never went to bed. I thanked, praised, washed, ironed, showered, packed, and left. I made it to the airport and flew out at 6 a.m. to sunny Arizona, where it was 80 degrees all week.

I was so grateful.

"No one is as capable of gratitude as the one who has emerged from the kingdom of night."[70] Elie Wiesel wrote, *"We know that every moment is a moment of grace, every hour an offering; not to share them would mean to betray them. Our lives no longer belong to us alone; they*

---

[70] Elie Wiesel. *The Night Trilogy #1: Night*. (New York: Bantam, 1982).

belong to all those who need us desperately."[71]

Ending this book with the conclusion of my stormy night would be unloving and unkind because many of you are still traveling through your night. Although I made it back home that stormy night in 2003, I still struggle with the night of OCD and how to navigate it. Although I have made great progress, it remains real and something I deal with by God's grace and help on an almost daily basis. His grace offered so generously during my dark times motivates me to encourage you through your night. He has not wasted my dark nights but used them to cultivate greater sensitivity and compassion within me for other fellow strugglers facing their nights. He has also used my own suffering to produce a heightened awareness of the perseverance it takes to get through a storm.

The best picture of a perfect storm and the perseverance it requires is found in Acts 27. Paul, one of many prisoners, and Julius, a centurion in charge, set sail for Rome to navigate a fourteen-day storm that scared them to death and nearly took their lives.

Paul writes that after putting the ship out to sea: *"The winds were against us"* (Acts 27:4). Sometimes, navigating the night can feel like everything is against us.

"We made slow headway for many days and had difficulty arriving..." (Acts 27:7a). Progress can be so difficult and slow that some days may feel like we are even moving backward.

"...the wind did not allow us to hold our course..." (Acts 27:7b). It is so disillusioning to get knocked off course and not know how or where to get back on. Severe disorientation can take place.

"Much time had been lost, and sailing had become

---

[71] Elie Wiesel. *The Night Trilogy #1: Night.* (New York: Bantam, 1982).

dangerous" (Acts 27:9).

"We took such a violent battering from the storm that the next day they began to throw the cargo overboard" (Acts 27:18). Dark nights can batter the soul and cause us to do drastic things.

"When neither sun nor stars appeared for many days and the storm continued raging, we finally <u>gave up all hope</u> of being saved" (Acts 27:20).

Notice the overwhelming temptation to quit or give up in the storm. Navigating the night for many days can create an obsession to quit, give up, throw in the towel, jump overboard, shrink back, or become hopeless. We desire to end our suffering or reach a conclusion at any cost, even if it isn't the one we want.

Paul knew the seriousness of this temptation for all those on board, and he offered them strong encouragement: *"But now I urge you to keep up your courage, because not one of you will be lost; only the ship will be destroyed"* (Acts 27:22). Scripture lets us know that an angel of God delivered this good news to Paul who passionately announced it to his fellow passengers (Acts 27:23-26). I want you to hear what Paul said again, *"But now I urge you to keep up your courage..."* **When we navigate the night, we must cling to courage, and we must get unhooked from the thought of quitting.**

As they say in the country, the most important thing to quit during dark times is **"to quit your quittin!"**[72]

Some tried to escape, but Paul said to the centurion and the soldiers, *"Unless these men stay with the ship, you cannot be saved"* (Acts 27:31)

"...and they prayed for daylight" (Acts 27:29). It eventually

---

[72] Newton Metzger. *A Treasury of Folklore and Humor*, 30.

came. *"When daylight came, they did not recognize the land..."* (Acts 27:39).

"...everyone reached land in safety" (Acts 27:44).

Remember, there will always be many voices in the night, including a lot of unworthy, dishonorable, and despicable voices that say: *"Jump off!" "Give up!" "Quit!" "You don't have what it takes!" "Things will never change!"* These thoughts have tormented me during severe bouts of religious scrupulosity.

It is tempting to abandon trust in dark times. Don't! If you were riding a train through a dark tunnel, you wouldn't jump off into the dark, would you? No! You would stay on board and trust the conductor to guide you through the dark tunnel. God is your conductor, guiding you through the night. Trust Him!

I often pray when I feel tired and weary, *"Lord, grant me a willing spirit, to sustain me"* (Psalm 51:12b). I want to be one of your willing ones! Help me not quit, but receive Your quickening Spirit!

James, the half-brother of Jesus, encouraged a multitude of Jewish Christians scattered among the nations because of their faith. Many had been displaced from their country, family, home, jobs, and any sense of normalcy, and they were tempted to lose all hope. James gave them this word of encouragement in their dark night: *"Blessed is the man who <u>perseveres</u> under trial, because when he has stood the test, he will receive the crown of life that God has promised to those who love Him..."* (James 1:12).

The Greek word for perseveres is *hupomone*, pronounced hoo-paw-maw-nay, which means *"to remain (with faith in God) under a heavy load."* This is one Greek word that needs to be in every believer's vocabulary! A heavy load calls for a strong faith in God. James reminded Jesus' followers not to give up their faith in God during the night seasons but to ask God to take them deeper in their faith in Him.

Hupomone suggests three primary qualities:

1. <u>Active Endurance</u>

Believers are called to actively endure, not just to passively survive. James is blissfully upbeat in his encouragement to scattered believers to have an unshakable, unsinkable spirit of blazing hope and joy when they face trials because of their assurance that God is at work in them improving, maturing, and fulfilling.

In high school, I ran competitive cross country, which included completing a three-mile foot race without stopping. Cross country is not for sissies! Every race required total focus and fortitude. Every course came with difficult terrain, agonizing hills, obstacles of extreme hot or cold weather, and strong competition. When my leg muscles tightened, my heart pounded, my mouth dried as cotton, and burning sweat ran into my eyes, I often had to resist the voice of pain that shouted, *"Quit!"*

Hebrews 12 compares the Christian life to running a race: *"Let us run with perseverance the race marked out for us"* (Hebrews 12:1). We must not forget that among the voices of the night during this race is also the voice of our Savior saying, *"Keep on running!" "You're almost there!" "Stay on board!"* His voice is the one we need to wholeheartedly listen for, tune into and respond to because it leads to hope and new life. We can recognize His voice because it always urges us to trust Him regardless of how difficult our circumstances are. It doesn't condemn us but invites us to choose the courage to live. Kristian Stanfill's album, *Make It Out Alive*, includes a song entitled "That's Not You," with some wonderful lyrics that help us discern between the voice of truth and many others in the night:

"I don't annoy You when I'm calling out Your name

I'm not a burden to You or just some charity case
You won't hide from me or tell me to go away
If I feel that, that's not You

That's not You at my lowest
Making sure I remember
Every single failure
All the times I missed the mark
That's not You in my weakness
Telling me I'm not worth it
And the race that I've been running
I should just give it up
That's not Your voice, that's not the truth
That's not You
Jesus that's not You
Jesus that's not You
Oh, that's not You
Oh, that's not You

You don't make a promise then go change Your mind
You don't tell me to stay away 'til I clean up my life
You never make me question if I should be alive
If I hear that, that's not You

There's a difference between the life You bring
And the lies the darkness speaks
There's a war inside this heart of mine
God, help me to see"[73]

Followers of Jesus must listen to God's voice of truth and push through their pain by taking it to Him, not by trying to bench-press it on their own. "Cast your burden on the Lord, and He will sustain you; He will never permit the righteous to be moved" (Psalm 55:22 ESV).

We must cling to the courage to persevere, knowing that something better lies ahead. The pain might not go away,

---

[73] Kristian Stanfill. "That's Not You." Track 3 on *Make It Out Alive*. Six Steps Records/Sparrow Records. 2022.

nor the outcome always be what we want, but God will sustain us and help us get back on course. Our pain is part of our potential and awareness of our weakness that helps us discover our true strength.

The writer of Hebrews describes the way Jesus faced the Cross, *"who for the joy set before Him endured the Cross"* (Hebrews 12:2). Our Savior faced the Cross with blazing hope and joy. **He didn't give up, but gave Himself up to the Father out of love for Him and us.** Before we impulsively jump ship, quit, or give up, we need to consider the people who are counting on us to continue with the Lord to the finish line. **We need to keep going for the sake of love.**

I never won a race, but thankfully, I never quit a race either and that's a win! The people who counted on me inspired me to push through the pain as part of love. My coach, Jon Chew, loved me and invested in me even when he was battling cancer that eventually took his life. I had a brother, Chad, who ran encouragingly by my side, and I was blessed with a band of brothers who trained with me. We counted on each other. As hard as cross country was, it can't compare to life. The tests since then have been far greater than I could ever have imagined. But so are the victories! I have far more reasons not to quit than ever before – the Lord who died for me and a host of people who love me and count on me remain at the top of my list. **The Lord and many others are counting on you too! I am counting on you.**

The primary way I am counting on you is to be humble and wise enough not to run the race of life alone. If you are used to isolation, you MUST step out of your self-contained world of survival and seek help. Refuse to live a life of quiet desperation. Go for help! Each of us needs help from someone who sees our potential and knows how to bring it out. This might be a pastor, mentor, counselor, physician, life coach, seasoned older adult, or wise friend. We also need a brother or sister or two who run closely by our side, cheerleaders who encourage us to keep running through the pain with our eyes fixed on Christ. Lastly, we all need community, a band of sisters or brothers who are counting on us to run to the finish line. **Who is your coach, friend, and community?**

John 11 tells the story of Lazarus' death and his being raised from the dead. Jesus did the raising but then turned to the community around Lazarus and said, *"(You) take off the grave clothes and let him go"* (11:43-44). The community unwrapped Lazarus so he could move and live again. God calls others to be part of His restoring team in our lives, to help us get unhooked and unstuck from what holds us or binds us. He also calls us to be part of this unwrapping ministry for the sake of others.

Running in community often prevents us from staying bound and possibly giving up. Sometimes we do give up, and we need the community to give us a hand up and help restore us for the next race.

In 1952, Florence Chadwick, a female swimmer, attempted a 26-mile swim across part of the English Channel. At the time, this was one of the toughest endurance tests in the world. After swimming for nearly 15 hours, a thick fog began to set in, clouding Chadwick's vision and confidence. She was also battling frigid water and nearby sharks that her crew shot at to keep them away. With just half a mile away from land, she gave up. Later she told a reporter, *"Look, I'm not excusing myself, but if I could have seen the land, I might have made it."*[74]

So often, we fail to realize that we are closer than we think. We simply quit too early.

2. Patient Persistence

Most people have a can of WD-40 around the house. The

---

[74] Nick Maccarone. *Emphasis Magazine*, January 8, 2018.

letters "WD" stand for "Water Displacement." The "40" is how many times the scientists tried to develop an effective formula. They failed 39 times but succeeded on the 40th try. The Message is: DON'T GIVE UP. Don't quit when you are tired. Don't quit when you fail. Don't quit when you are facing insurmountable obstacles.

Paul said, *"Let us not become weary in doing good, for at the proper time (in due season) we will reap a harvest if we do not quit"* (Galatians 6:9).

An unknown author once said, **"The greatest oak was once a little nut that held its ground."**

The great Oriental conqueror, Tamerlane, once told his friends, *"Observe the ant."* In sharing a story from his early life, he said, "I once was forced to take shelter from my enemies in a dilapidated building, where I sat alone for many hours. Wishing to divert my mind from my hopeless situation, I fixed my eyes on an ant carrying a kernel of corn larger than itself up a high wall. I counted its efforts to accomplish this feat."

"The corn fell sixty-nine times to the ground, but the insect persevered. The seventieth time it reached the top. The ant's accomplishment gave me the courage for the moment, and I never forgot the lesson."[75]

The genius physicist, Albert Einstein, once said, **"It's not that I'm so smart; it's just that I stay with problems longer."**[76]

Perseverance requires persistence. Two months after Florence Chadwick failed to swim 26 miles of the English Channel, she tried again. Once again, a thick fog set in, but this time she had the mental image of the shoreline in her mind as she pushed herself along. She not only succeeded

---

[75] L.B. Cowman, *Streams in the Desert* (Chump Change Publishers, 1925), 38-39
[76] "Albert Einstein Quotes" GoodReads.com. Accessed from http://www.goodreads.com.

this time but also completed it two more times.

David is convinced that no matter how long the dark night, *"that my God will turn my darkness into light"* (Psalm 18:28). But the miracle of transformation requires us to cooperate with God by patiently persisting again and again.

The writer of Hebrews 10 encourages those who suffer: *"So do not throw away your confidence; it will be richly rewarded. You need to persevere so that when you have done the will of God, you will receive what He has promised"* (Hebrews 10:35-36).

God Himself is the grandest reason not to give up. *"Let us hold unswervingly to the hope we profess, for He who promised is faithful"* (Hebrews 10:23). We rest and continue in God's faithfulness.

3. Daily Entrusting

Part of the idea of *hupomone* involves daily entrusting our lives to God.

Our lives are made up of days – all kinds of days – earlier days, present days, days to come, cloudy days, rainy days, and sunny days. **Every day, come fair or foul weather, on our best days and our worst days, we decide to stay on board, to endure and persist in full assurance of faith.**

David declared: *"But I trust in you, O Lord...My times are in Your hands"* (Psalm 31:14a, 15a).

"Let us draw near to God with a sincere heart in full assurance of faith." - Hebrews 10:22

Oswald Chambers penned this call to daily trust most eloquently: *"Perseverance means more than endurance –*

more than simply holding on until the end. A saint's life is in the hands of God like a bow and arrow in the hands of an archer. God is aiming at something the saint cannot see, but our Lord continues to stretch and strain, and every once in a while, the saint says, 'I can't take it anymore.' Yet, God goes on stretching until His purpose is in sight, and then He lets the arrow fly. Entrust yourself to God's hands."[77]

I saw it with my own eyes. I am sure some of you saw it too – that heart-pounding 100-meter butterfly swim duel between Serbia's Milorad Cavic and USA's Michael Phelps in the 2008 Olympics. Had it not been for the advanced electronic touch pads, it may have been impossible to declare a winner. Phelps won *"by a fingernail"* one commentator enthusiastically reported. The replay showed that the leading Cavic relaxed his stroke heading into the wall, unlike Phelps, who stretched his stroke and *"swam through to the wall."*

As I watched in wonder, I asked myself if I am committed to swim to the wall – to finish well no matter what challenges I face. I ask you that question too. Are you committed to swim to the wall, sing the note out, follow through on the pitch, and stay on board all the way to shore?

We are so tempted to give up right before the victory. So many victories have been prevented because we give up just a little too soon. Medals meant for us hang around someone else's neck. So often, the difference between victory and defeat is continuing. Some keep on. Some quit. Remember that God's blessings come to those who stand the test.

---

[77] Oswald Chambers. "May 8th: The Faith to Persevere." *My Utmost for His Highest: An Updated Edition in Today's Language* (Grand Rapids: Discovery House Publishers, 1992).

"...when he has stood the test, he will receive the crown of life that God has promised to those who love Him." - James 1:12b-c

---

The benefits of standing the test are out of this world!

In this life, we become people of genuine worth. Like purified gold, our weaknesses are tried by fire and transformed or eradicated altogether (1 Peter 1:7). We become authentically and increasingly God's for His praise and the sake of others.

In the life to come, we receive the crown of life, a phrase that carries rich biblical imagery of great celebration. James' audience could see:

a. A crown of flowers worn on joyful occasions such as weddings and feasts. We are about ready to party!
b. A crown of royalty worn by kings and those in authority. We are about ready to rule with Christ!
c. A crown of victory worn by athletes who finish the contest. We are about ready to cross the finish line to victory!
d. A crown of honor worn by those to whom God says, *"Well done, thy good and faithful servant..."* (Matthew 25:21).
e. A crown of life that represents a new kind of abundant living that is offered and experienced in Jesus Christ.

And these descriptions just scratch the surface of all God intends for those who love Him.

"No eye has seen, no ear has heard, no mind has conceived what God has prepared for those who love Him." - 1 Corinthians 2:9

No matter what we go through in this life, be reassured that it's worth being a person of faith and hope. Teresa of Avila, a saint from the 16th century, puts our earthly suffering in perspective when she writes **"from heaven the most miserable earthly life will look like one bad night at an inconvenient hotel."**[78]

"Weeping may remain for a night; but rejoicing comes in the morning." - Psalm 30:5b

---

Irish poet, John O'Donohue, writes:

"If you have ever had the occasion to be out early in the morning before the dawn breaks, you will have noticed that the darkest time of night is immediately before dawn. The darkness deepens and becomes more anonymous. If you have never been to the world and never known what a day was, you couldn't possibly imagine how the darkness breaks, how the mystery and color of a new day arrives. Light is incredibly generous, but also gentle. When you attend to the way the dawn comes, you learn how light can coax the dark."[79] **Light gently overtakes the darkness and has the last word!**

Francis de Sales, a French saint born in the 16th century, expresses the beauty and mystery of the light and encourages us to keep on going with God and never give up:

"The rising of devotion in an ordinary soul is like the dawning of a new day. Darkness is not driven away immediately. Light comes in small increments, moment by moment. The saying is that a slow cure is best. Sicknesses of the soul are like those of the body. They come galloping

---

[78] "Teresa of Avila Quotes." Accessed from http://www.inspiringquotes.us.
[79] John O'Donohue. *Anam Cara* (London: Bantam Press, 1997), 21.

in on horseback but depart slowly on foot. **Have courage and be patient.** *Many see themselves as still imperfect after trying to be devout for a long time. They become discouraged and are tempted to give up. The opposite temptation is far more hazardous. Some figure everything is fixed on the first day! They have scarcely begun. They want to fly without wings. They are taking a great risk of relapse if they stop seeing the doctor too soon."*[80]

"Even in darkness light dawns for the upright, for the gracious and compassionate and righteous man."
- Psalm 112:4

"I will give you the treasures of darkness and riches hidden in secret places, that you may know that it is I, the Lord, the God of Israel, who call you by your name." - Isaiah 45:3 NRSV[81]

There is coming a day when *"**there will be no more night**. His servants will not need the light of a lamp or the light of the sun, for the Lord God will give them light. And they will reign for ever and ever"* (Revelation 22:5).

Keep up your courage. Don't quit. Don't give up. Stay on Board.

---

[80] Bernard Bangley. *Nearer to the Heart of God: Daily Readings with the Christian Mystics* (Brewster: Paraclete Press, 2005), 29.
[81] THE HOLY BIBLE: NEW REVISED STANDARD VERSION (Nashville: Thomas Nelson Publishers, 1989).

Questions for Thought And Discussion

Chapter 6 – Stay on Board

1. Do you agree with Elie Wiesel's words that *"no one is as capable of gratitude as the one who has emerged from the kingdom of night?"*

2. Has God ever brought you through a dark time that left you with such overwhelming gratitude that you couldn't wait to share it with another fellow struggler to encourage them?

3. List the three characteristics of perseverance (hupomone):
   a. _____ endurance
   b. _____ persistence
   c. _____ entrusting

4. Would you describe yourself as more of a passive survivor or as an active endurer? Why?

5. Does it inspire you to persevere for the sake of love? Who is counting on you?

6. How can you discern the difference between God's voice of truth and lying voices of the night? (Look back at Kristian Stanfill's song "That's Not You").

7. Are you trapped in isolation and quiet desperation or are you free to ask for help?

8. Is it worth being a person of faith and hope? Why or why not?

9. Has this book made any positive difference in how you plan to live the rest of your life? If so, I would love to hear from you. You can contact me via email at chriscarter1218@gmail.com

Chapter 7
Next Steps

Perhaps you have been plunged into darkness and wonder if there is a next step. THERE IS! Before I share the hope of it, let me tell you what it is not. It is not found by ending your life, escaping from life, or creating your own rules for life. It is found in calling on the God of life, love, and light and moving toward Him. It is found in taking your pain to Him in whatever ways you struggle. There is no problem beyond His grace and help.

"For everyone who calls on the name of the Lord will be saved" (Romans 10:13). The King James Version says, *"Whosoever..."*

The next step is always to move toward God. If you are not a believer, I encourage you to openly explore the exclusive claims of Christ to be the way, the truth, and the life (John 14:6a). He says, *"No one comes to the Father except through Me"* (John 14:6b). I am thoroughly convinced that Jesus is the way to the Father and cannot imagine my life apart from Him. He helps me live by faith and find hope in every dark night.

When I am weary in any way, I remember Jesus' words: *"**Come to Me**, all you who are weary and burdened, and I will give you rest. Take My yoke upon you and **learn from Me**, for I am gentle and humble in heart, and you will find rest for your souls. For my yoke is easy and my burden is light"* (Matthew 11:28-30).

Isaiah prophesied about the Messiah seven hundred years before He came to earth. He said the Messiah would be born a child to dawn as a light upon those walking in darkness and in the shadow of death (Isaiah 9:2). Jesus Himself said, *"I am the light of the world. Whoever follows Me will never walk in darkness but will have the light of life"* (John 8:12). We may experience or battle the darkness, but it will not define us or overcome us if we are in Christ. It may appear to have the upper hand, but God will have the last word.

Perhaps you are a believer, but you realize you have been so problem-centered or project centered, that you have stopped acting like it. You have forgotten to look to the Lord altogether. Your belief is mental assent, but you don't entrust your daily life and all its details to Him. You know about Him but do not practice the means of grace that help you experience His presence. You realize that you have become deaf and blind, and you want to come home to the Father. He is waiting with a welcoming embrace!

"When we get waylaid from our walk with God by busyness, depression, OCD, family problems, or worse, God does not abandon us."[82]

Lastly, you may be a strong believer, but God seems absent to you right now. You wonder what you've done. You feel nothing but the pain of your disconnectedness and weaknesses. You are struggling to see. Keep moving towards God. Keep meeting with Him. Keep expressing your desire to love Him above all. Keep inviting Him to have His way with you. Keep depending on Him. Trust God with your feelings even if they feel dead. Part of faith is trusting God's faithfulness even when we feel nothing.

Sarah Young, in her brilliant devotional, *Jesus Calling*, shares some things she believes God says to believers navigating the night. Hear these words personally from the Father to you: *"In this age of independence, people find it hard to acknowledge their neediness. However, I have taken you along a path that has highlighted your need for Me, placing you in situations where your strengths were irrelevant, and your weaknesses were glaringly evident...You have realized that needing Me is the key to*

---

[82] Brennan Manning. *Ruthless Trust: The Ragamuffin's Path to God* (New York: Harper Collins, 2000), 19.

knowing Me intimately." [83]

Lastly, sometimes we need to talk to another person about what we are going through. Be courageous to be humble and wise enough not to run this race alone. Step out of your self-contained world of survival and seek help. Refuse to live a life of quiet desperation. Go for help! Find a deeply devoted disciple of Jesus to walk with you.

Please contact me if I can be a listening and encouraging friend at chriscarter1218@gmail.com

---

[83] Sarah Young. *Jesus Calling* (Nashville: Thomas Nelson, 2004), 348.

NIGHT LIGHTS
Devotions for the Heart

I remember as a boy growing up the joy of having an overnight visitor or guest in our home. It was always so exciting. Mom always made sure our guests were as comfortable as possible. She cooked great meals for them, put on clean sheets, made sure their room was tidy, and always provided a night light. My wife instinctively does the very same thing. She creates a warm and friendly environment!

When we are in our own homes, we are familiar enough with them and have enough experience navigating them to almost feel our way through, even in the dark, but when we are in an unfamiliar place, we need a little extra light in the night to find our way. Some of us find ourselves in very unfamiliar places. I pray the short devotions that follow will serve as night lights for your heart.

God with Us

"Let the light of your face shine upon us, O Lord."
Psalm 4:6b

I had a dream. I was in an endless forest of towering trees. In every direction I looked, there was more forest. A forest can be dark and scary, full of wild animals, crawling reptiles and insects, poisonous plants, and the paralyzing fear of not knowing how to turn to get home.

Amid my panicking, pressured heart, I saw Jesus. He stepped out towards me from behind one of the trees with hands open wide. He had a look of delightful surprise as He could hardly wait to reveal Himself. He had the friendliest face, His eyes filled with compassionate light. As He peered through me, I felt the joy of having a friend who fully understood me and unconditionally loved me. The weight of worry fell off my troubled shoulders.

Sometimes, we feel like a Cherokee Indian youth moving into manhood. The tribe had a custom of taking him into the middle of the woods on a dark night and leaving him alone in deep darkness. His skin would crawl as he heard every owl hoot, every branch rustle, every falling pinecone, and every scurrying rodent. He imagined every shadow as a black bear looking for a meal. He struggled through a terror-filled night, anxiously awaiting the comfort of dawn. Sometimes our souls feel like a dark and scary night of aloneness.

But what happened at dawn? As the young Cherokee strained his eyes to see his surroundings more clearly, one of the first things he would see was his father standing watch nearby with weapons, ready to protect him. The boy becoming a man realized his father was with him all night.

And our Father is with us in Jesus in every forest and every night. He is Immanuel, God with us (Matthew 1:23). He is close and at ease in every forest because He is the Master of the Sea and land and every living thing.

May the light of His face shine on you! He will protect and guide you through the night to home.

In Praise of His Presence with us,
Brother Chris

Sunshine on My Shoulders

"...the rising sun will come to us from heaven to shine on those living in darkness."
Luke 1:78

Recently a dear friend shared with me that his precious wife suffered from SAD (Seasonal Affective Disorder). The absence of sunshine for long periods of time during cold, dark winters can bury hope in some hearts.

Although most of us have never been diagnosed with such a disorder, we all know what it is to feel SAD. I woke this morning feeling a bit blue, down on myself, like I needed a good nap and a full day of nothing to do. MY FAVORITE THING TO DO IS NOTHING! But I had lots to do, so I prayed God would help me. His grace and a little discipline helped my feet hit the floor.

My first stop of the day was the gas station. With my cold hands shaking and my body shivering, I pumped gas in the cloudy, below-freezing temperature, staring at the miracle of snow all around me. It was beautiful, but I still felt like I needed to go back to bed. But in a split second, something phenomenal happened – a break in the clouds.

The sun broke through. I felt the warmth of heaven's sun shining on my shoulders. It felt so good. Sunshine on my shoulders makes me happy. Luke 1 records Zechariah, the priest's song of praise for the coming Messiah, whom he described as the rising sun from heaven. Jesus has overcome darkness and the shadow of death. And He will break through the clouds in our lives and restore us repeatedly until that great day when all sin and sadness will melt away.

He's coming back. Until then, may the presence of the shining sun remind us of the Son who is about ready to break through the clouds. When Jesus comes again, *"He will wipe away every tear. There will be no more death or mourning or crying or pain, for the old order of things has passed away!"* (Revelation 21:4).

Looking for Him and Trusting our Lord to breakthrough your clouds,
Brother Chris

Waiting in Prayer

"I wait for the Lord, my soul waits, and in His Word, I put my hope."
Psalm 130:5

Waiting at a traffic light irritates us because we can't make it change. Waiting for an appointment annoys us because we can't speed up the clock. Waiting for a bus bothers us because we cannot control its movement. Waiting for a response causes insecurity because we see it as love withheld. Prayer is something else.

We are no longer in control when we pray. God is in control. He will come when He thinks it is time to come and in the way He thinks best. Although the world always needed God's Son, the Father sent Him to earth only in *"the fullness of time"* (Galatians 4:4). Solomon reminds us that *"there is a time for everything"* (Ecclesiastes 3:1). His timing is part of His love. I love the old chorus, *"In His Time,"* which assures us that our Lord makes all things beautiful in His time, not ours. Our waiting can be filled with hopeful expectation or panic that sends us striving to control outcomes.

Because we serve a covenant-making God, we can wait with open hands rather than clenched fists. We can abide rather than strive. We can wait hopefully for the Lord and in the promises of His Word. We must remember that we aren't waiting alone but that He is with us in our waiting! He desires to calm our fears as a loving parent settles a tired or tearful toddler.

I love the encouragement of one writer who says, *"Prayer is the courage to listen, to give up self-determination...it implies waiting – as before any birth – in darkness and expectancy."*[84] Let's bring our seasons of waiting to the Lord and imagine Him weaving our circumstances together

---

[84] Peter G. Van Breemen. *As Bread That is Broken* (Denville: Dimension Books, 1974), 42-43.

to fulfill His wonderful plan.

If you are in a season of waiting, wait with hope!

Waiting in the Word,
Brother Chris

Bright Lights

"You are the light of the world...let your light shine before others, so that they may see...and praise your Father in heaven."
Matthew 5:14, 16

Just before Christmas, I saw Teena Maginn, the associate head of our day school, walking down the hall with a strand of multi-colored lights flashing around her neck. She truly is a bright light! God calls and equips all Christians to be bright lights.

In every believer is a divine, life-giving spark! The spark is Christ Himself, who is our light. We have no light of our own unless Jesus shines through us. Not even death's darkness could extinguish His light. Our greatest reach into the lives of others doesn't come from what we preach or teach but how we live. The gospel is best communicated through our demeanor, not just our doctrine.

The credibility of the Church when it preaches God's love for the lost depends on whether the Church itself goes out to people in their lostness, identifies itself with them, and in a priestly way, makes their predicament its own. In the words of the holiness Irish preacher Robert Murray M'Cheyne, we need to pray to be the kind of Christians who make it easy for others to believe in God.[85] Our Father in heaven wants to give us more than a ticket to heaven but a transformed life while we are on our way! He wants to get into our mouths, our manners, and our motives and shine through us.

A.W. Tozer once posed this question: *"Aren't all Christians*

---

[85] "Robert Murray M'Cheyne Quotes." Accessed from http://www.allchristianquotes.org.

alike?" Then he answered with a resounding *"No. Not all Christians are alike. Some shine like the stars in heaven – some big, some little, and some you must take a telescope to see."*

Prayer: Risen Lord, in the darkness of these winter months, make us bright lights for You. Transform our lives until others see You and You are praised!

For Greater Shining,
Brother Chris

Eternal Light

"You, O Lord, keep my lamp burning; my God turns my darkness into light"
Psalm 18:28

There is not a single road that we walk alone, especially the ones that seem the loneliest and darkest. I remember visiting Cumberland Caverns on an eighth-grade field trip. These caverns seemed endless as we middle schoolers wound our way through the cold, dark tunnels, nothing lighting our way but small flashlights. Our hands reached forward hoping to feel the person in front of us. Our journey is often like this, but in our case, God is always in front of us whether we feel Him or not. He keeps our lamps burning. He turns our darkness into light. He guides us through every tunnel.

I am aware of some of the dark times in your lives – the disappointments that don't make sense, the sticky places that are hard to maneuver, the waiting and waiting and waiting, the rejections, the detours that require you to begin again when you aren't sure if you can. God is ahead, turning darkness into light. Work and walk to the edge of your light, and there will be more light at just the right time!

Speaking of sticky places, I remember walking through "Bubble Gum Alley" named as such for the sticky, glue-like substance that lined the cave floor in a narrow, tight alley in the caverns. It was literally like walking on top of a bed of bubblegum. There was no way to walk fast because you spent so much time recovering or trying to free yourself from the last step. I learned that speed wasn't the important thing, rather an ongoing determination to take slow, intentional steps. Before long, I had walked into freedom, breaking through the stickiness of it all.

No problem or challenge in your life or mine is greater than our God. Be a determined disciple, not by gritting your teeth, but by holding to His Almighty Hand! May He light your way!

For encouragement in dark times and for light at the right time,

Brother Chris

An Honest Fellowship

"But if we confess our sins, He is faithful and just to forgive us our sins and cleanse us from everything we've done wrong."
1 John 1:9

In Jesus Christ, we are called to be a fellowship of light because *"God is light and there is no darkness in him at all"* (1:5). Our relationship with God and each other is to be based on honesty, not pretense or lies.

Some false teachers taught that believers could go on living in spiritual darkness and still have fellowship with God. But three times John uses the phrase "if we claim" to have fellowship with God but go on sinning, we are still living in the darkness (1:6, 8, & 10). Saying one thing and doing another is dangerous!

I heard a lady tell of taking her little boy fishing at a good friend's pond. Each time they used his small boat and would turn it upside down to drain the water until the next time they used it. No matter how short or long between trips, she said every time they turned it over, critters crawled out: bugs, beavers, and snakes. Darkness attracts things we really don't want in our lives.

An honest fellowship seeks to live right side up and let the light in. We do this through confession. When we expose our sins, Jesus' blood cleanses us, and we enjoy real relationship with Him and each other.

For More Light and Fellowship,
Brother Chris

In the Hands of the Father

"Into Your hands, I commit my spirit...My times are in Your hands."
Psalm 31:5a, 15a

Many winters ago, while still living at home with my parents my first year of college, a winter storm hit that made it impossible to leave our house for four days. Steep hills made our neighborhood impassable. The time came for me to return to school as roads in the valley were melting and getting easier to drive on.

Unfortunately, the only way out was a back entrance. I wasn't experienced at driving on ice and snow so my dad offered to lead me out with his car, and I could follow him in mine. So, I tried. My car felt like a top on that ice. I had no control. I made it over the first hill, but before I came to the second, I saw two ponds, one on each side of the road. I feared I might slide off into one of them and sink forever. By God's grace, I made it over the second hill. By this time, dad's car was out of sight. I came to the third hill and started spinning and turned sideways in the road. I froze along with my car – neither of us moved, and I liked it that way! But I was stuck and didn't know how to make any progress.

I looked up and saw my dad carefully walking over the hill towards my car. He was coming back after me. That brought some assurance. He finally reached the car and, with a patient and calm voice, told me to exchange seats with him. I willingly surrendered the steering wheel to him, and he guided me over that last hill.

In Carrie Underwood's hit song, "Jesus, Take the Wheel," a young mother is driving home in the winter snow with a baby in the backseat and a troubled heart. She breaks down emotionally and prays:

"Jesus, take the wheel
Take it from my hands
'Cause I can't do this on my own
I'm letting go
So, give me one more chance
And save me from this road I'm on
Jesus, take the wheel."[86]

There are times in all our lives when we are breaking down and don't know what to do. We have a choice to make. We can try to do it on our own or remember that we have a Heavenly Father who cares so much about us that He comes to us in the storm and guides us to safety. Put your life and everything in it in His hands.

For More Surrender,
Brother Chris

---

[86] Carrie Underwood. "Jesus, Take the Wheel." Track 4 on *Some Hearts*. 19 Recordings Limited. 2005.

About the Author

Chris Carter, better known by most as *"Brother Chris,"* has served as a pastor since 1988 in various roles: as a Senior Pastor, a Senior Associate Pastor, a Discipleship Pastor, a Hospice Chaplain, a Care Ministries Pastor, and currently as an Executive Pastor at Christ Church Memphis in Memphis, Tennessee where he has served the past eleven years.

Chris has bachelor's degrees in English Literature and Biblical Education from Lee University in Cleveland, Tennessee, and a Master of Divinity (MDiv) and Doctor of Ministry (DMin) in Biblical Preaching and Leadership from Asbury Theological Seminary in Wilmore, Kentucky.

Chris enjoys storytelling, singing, speaking, and writing in the areas of spiritual formation, pastoral care, and gerontology. His spiritual journey has been a convergence of different streams or traditions of the Christian faith. He describes himself as an "Evangelical Methocostal Mystic" and seeks to be a minister of encouragement in whatever role of ministry he finds himself.

Chris is married to Tonya and has four sons: Brady, Connor, Eli, and Buddy, the family's Border Collie. He enjoys reading, laughing, basketball, practicing the presence of God and people, and visiting the country. His favorite place is Cades Cove in the Great Smoky Mountains National Park near Gatlinburg, Tennessee.

If you desire to contact him, please write him at **chriscarter1218@gmail.com**

Made in United States
North Haven, CT
31 January 2023